TAKING NOTICE

How a Cancer Journey Helps
Magnify What's Important in Life

TAKING NOTICE

How a Cancer Journey Helps
Magnify What's Important in Life

Rick Bergh, M.Div., CT

Author of *Finding Anchors* and *Looking Ahead*

Taking Notice

Published by
Beacon Mount Publishing
#18 West Chapman Place
Cochrane, Alberta, T4C 1J9, Canada
www.rickbergh.com

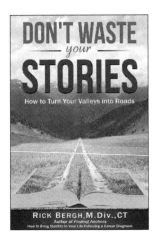

Go to www.rickbergh.com/
dontwasteyourstories
for your free copy

ISBN 978-0-9947962-6-4 (paperback)
ISBN 978-1-988082-09-7 (hardcover)
ISBN 978-1-988082-03-5 (audio)
ISBN 978-1-988082-01-1 (ePub)
ISBN 978-1-988082-06-6 (Mobi)

Author's Note
Names, details and circumstances may have been changed to protect the privacy of those mentioned in this book.

The publication contained in this book is not intended as a substitute for the advice of health care professionals.

Printed and bound in the United States of America.

Dedication

This book is dedicated to our four children, Devon, Keeara, Larissa and Landon.

And to Pam, their mom, who taught each of us to live life to the fullest in the midst of her cancer journey.

Acknowledgements

The stories in this book are true. They take place over a five-year time period. It has taken another seven years to distill the insights we gained as a family and to put them in "pen and ink" for others to consider. I learned some powerful lessons as a result of our cancer journey with Pam. In looking back, I was surprised how they have now become the new bedrock principles to how I live life and find joy, purpose and meaning.

We started our cancer journey as a family in Westlock, Alberta. Thank you to that wonderful community for their care and support.

Our journey continued following a move to Cochrane, Alberta. Our new family at St. Peter's Lutheran Church provided a perfect place for our family to be surrounded by a group of loving and warm people. Thank you.

Thank you to my Mom and Dad. I needed them in my life and their unwavering support, encouragement and prayers flowed daily into our lives.

To my other Mom and Dad, Pam's parents, and a host of relatives on both sides of the family—thank you all. We felt so blessed by your support during our up-and-down journey.

I knew I wanted to write these thoughts down on paper, but I did not know where to start. I want to give a big shout-out to Steve and Bill Harrison for their amazing programs. The *Quantum Leap Publishing* program was the key in helping me get started. Thank you.

I want to thank my editor, Rhonda Fleming of RJF Writing Services, for her wisdom, guidance and patience. Thank you for believing in my work.

I want to thank Erica, my wife, who pushed me to write this story and all of the books in this series. She is my biggest cheerleader. Thank you for helping me consider my other books in this series. You are an amazing wife and loved deeply by me.

Thank you, God, for never leaving me. I can't say I trusted You fully all the time. You and I had some pretty deep and gut-wrenching conversations. Sometimes I felt You were listening while at other times, I wondered where You were. I didn't always trust you. I'm sorry. You were always by my side, as You promised. I thank you for teaching me through Pam what I needed to learn in my life. It seems I needed a lot of shaping by the Master Carpenter.

Contents

Preface

Last summer I built a sandbox for our grandchildren. I bought bags of sand to fill it up so we could play together. I love sand. One of my favorite things is walking in the sand in bare feet along a body of water.

I'm sure you know there are a lot of different colors of sand. But did you know that every grain of sand is unique, just like every snowflake that falls from the sky?

Once magnified, simple sand that we play with in our hands, or walk on with our feet, or look at with our eyes, becomes extraordinary in its shape, size, and color. I never would have thought that the sand I enjoy so much in Maui would look like the grains of sand on this book cover when placed beneath a magnifying glass.

As my wife Pam stepped out into her new life with cancer, I began to notice that what I had once seen as so ordinary became extraordinary. As a result, I began to see and live life differently.

Although this is mostly my story as a husband, the real story is what Pam unconsciously taught me in the midst of her cancer journey. She would never tell this story. She was much too humble. But I will, because I believe it can help others who may be entering this unfamiliar territory.

This book begins three months into Pam's cancer journey. She had been diagnosed with third stage ovarian cancer. She had gone through a complete hysterectomy and was close to completing her first round of chemotherapy treatments.

We had stabilized our family life and the initial shock of having a mom with cancer had subsided. We were doing the best we could to manage and live day-to-day with the changes that come as a result of cancer in a family.

And then I began to take notice.

I hope this book will encourage you. If you are reading this book as the one who has cancer, I want you to know that you are much more than someone who has cancer. You are teaching others about what is important in life. We need to sit at your feet and learn.

If you are companioning someone who has cancer, know that you are in a position to be changed and you need to take notice of what is most important in your life.

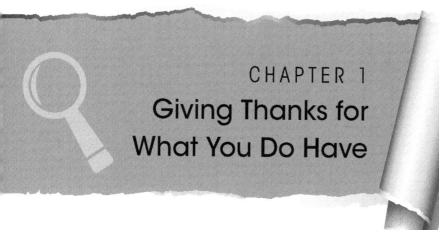

CHAPTER 1
Giving Thanks for What You Do Have

Thank you, God, for this good life and forgive us if we do not love it enough.

— GARRISON KEILLOR

I arrived at the church for my first Sunday as their new pastor and noticed there was a large clock hanging on the back wall. It was opposite the pulpit where I would stand to preach. It quickly became evident to me that the only person who could see the clock during the worship service was the preacher—in this case, me. I already knew that, for most people in this little church, staying on time was important and the positioning of the clock confirmed that. The previous pastor had, on average, 14-point sermons—so I understood what the congregation was telling me without them having to say a word.

Time is important. It's the most precious gift we have. Every life is terminal. We will all die someday. When cancer barged into our family's life, I began to come to a new understanding of the timeframe of both life and death. We don't know the time of our death, so we had better not pretend we have control of that part of our lives. But we can consider what we do with the minutes we've been given.

I've spent hours with people in hospice, waiting for them to take their last breath. It makes you appreciate every breath. It means *life*. It means *right now*. It means that life is not over yet. However, the truth is, every breath you breathe in and breathe out takes you closer to your final breath on this earth.

The significance of life took on a new meaning each time I watched my wife come out of her chemo treatments. *This had better work!* I'd say to myself. Sometimes late at night, when Pam was sleeping, I would wake up and simply watch her breathe. The magnificence of that experience was profound for me. When you breathe, you are living—you are still in this world. The minutes matter. The breaths matter.

Live like you're dying. That may seem like a simplistic principle, but I don't believe people really consider it until their back is against the wall. Everything would change if we did that and appreciated the gift of life that is given to each of us every day. Learning to appreciate life helped me take a closer look at the minutes of my day and what I was doing with them.

When you live with someone who has cancer, you feel like you're on the end of a bungee cord. You're never on solid ground. You're always dangling. It isn't pleasant, but it definitely demands something new of you that maybe you did not consider before. The minutes really are important. And there is no reason to waste time on things that are not significant or necessary.

Robin died. He was eight years old—a young, energetic boy. He went out one day and did what most young kids like to do: he rode his bike. A truck hit him and he was dead three days later. It rocked our little community. It was so unfair. It was so unexpected. The time was not right. His Dad said, "I wish I could have spent more time with my son."

Pam got cancer. It was not right. She was young, lived well, ate healthy, loved people, had no history of cancer in her family, and was outside the usual age bracket for ovarian cancer. Overnight, life for us changed.

Have you ever looked back on your day, your month or your year and asked this question: "Would I have lived those minutes differently if I could have?" Sometimes life seems to run away from us and we don't often have time to really consider what's significant or meaningful.

For me, the minutes became more special because of the uncertainty of our future. Cancer always has odds. The prognoses vary depending upon what type of cancer you have and what stage it is. These are not widely spoken about because it takes away hope. And we need to live in a place of hope.

My life is not my own. It's a gift given to me. I had nothing to do with my birth. I have little choice as to when and how I will die. But I have everything to do with how I live.

This is both sobering and empowering. Why empowering? Because when I begin to see my life and my finiteness for what it is, I discover my role in it more purposefully.

My daughter and her boyfriend decided to trek through some pretty rough countries in Latin America and I questioned her on her destinations of choice. "Dad, I have everything in place. If something happens to me, my records are all in this envelope. If I don't see you back here, I will see you in heaven." This same daughter is heading to the Middle East as I write this book, taking every minute to enjoy her life and this world to the fullest. She watched how her mom lived life, counting every minute as a gift given — she made no assumptions about the minutes, hours and days she had left. We are not *entitled* to life. It is a gift for which to say "thank you." When you see life from that perspective, you will no longer answer "same old same old" to the question, "How was your day?"

Every day is a day of grace. We can only know the truth of this statement when we know and believe that every life is terminal. Every moment counts.

Pam used to say constantly, "I'm so thankful." Sometimes I was confused because she was a pretty sick girl at times. What I noticed was that she even gave thanks for what she *didn't* have. Because we didn't know her future, the minutes counted.

There are many people who say they live one day at a time. They say they seize the day, that they make the most of it. But are people truly thankful for each day and what it gives them, even when it is not the perfect day they had hoped for?

Living life to the fullest means appreciating what you *do* have that's wonderful right now and not complaining when you don't get what you hoped for. It's not about living in a place of entitlement.

The importance of this concept was reinforced to me this past week when the daughter of a dear friend gave birth to a beautiful, healthy baby boy—one day after she was diagnosed with stage three cancer.

As I visited with them, I watched this young mom cuddle her baby boy and saw the miraculous gift of life and breath. What news do you share first with family and friends? The good news of new life! Yes, that little family may have a challenging journey ahead—or not. But they are choosing to celebrate what they do have—a baby—and not what they don't have—perfect health for Mommy.

It's a good day to be alive. You are living and breathing! Is that not enough?

CHAPTER 2
When Life Becomes Bigger Than the Cottage

I've always thought anyone can make money. Making a life worth living, that's the real test.

— ROBERT FULGHUM

his morning, during a long walk, I was reminded of an old injury I incurred a number of years ago. The injury happened while I was putting the final touches on a skylight on the roof of our cabin and I fell from the scaffolding.

I didn't quite break my ankle, but stretched the ligaments badly and was in a cast for a few months. The doctor said it would have been better if I had actually broken the ankle. A complete break would have been easier to treat. He remarked, "You will feel it from time to time now. It will never be the same." When I "felt" my ankle injury this morning, I recalled once again the doctor's words and how the accident had happened. But the injury was for the greater good. It was so we could enjoy our family cottage — together.

I bought a bare lake lot when our youngest son, Landon, was a year old. Even though I lived on a stipend as a pastor and Pam was a stay-at-home mom with four kids, I was determined to give our family a place where we could relax, have fun and enjoy each other. We also planned for the lakefront cabin to be Pam's and my retirement home.

Perspective is relative and often comes through the back door as you are comfortably seated in your proverbial easy chair. Cancer forced its way in while I was sitting in my easy chair. Then all of a sudden, life became bigger than the cottage we valued so much.

If you had to give up the most important material possession in your life, what would it be? Mine was the cabin, no doubt about it. I was proud of my accomplishments. I had sacrificed so much to build that dream cabin for our family.

Truthfully, I like material possessions. I like having things. Most of us do. We work hard to have things to enjoy. I loved our cottage. I had bought the land, and began building it with the little extra money that came in. It wasn't easy. Pam began to substitute teach a little as the kids got older, but we had very little cash left over at the end of the month. But everything that was left over went directly into building that cabin.

The cabin was an awesome getaway for our family. We spent summer after summer at this wonderful place, building a little more each year. This cottage was very special to us. And it was my pride and joy. I spent many hours away from Pam and the kids during those years trying to complete it myself, because we couldn't afford to hire others to work on it.

It wasn't just a cottage. We built it for the future. It was a place to retire. It would be big enough for grandchildren. It was heaven on earth for us. It was a place of amazing memories.

I will never forget one particular morning at the cottage. Pam was in her housecoat with a broom in her hand, chasing the geese off our sandy beach. The geese had decided to deposit their "little nuggets" for us on the beach and it was a ton of work to clean it up. We looked out the window to watch Mom scream at these geese and charge at them with her broom. A few seconds later, however, the largest goose reciprocated and began chasing Pam back onto the deck! We laughed. She laughed. The geese left. Ah! Cottage life!

Then cancer came. The woman with whom I wanted to spend the rest of my life had a body that was fighting for life and health. My focus was quickly directed away from the cottage and onto something much deeper. My wife.

Has that ever happened to you? You spent a lot of time, money and energy on something and it didn't work out. Or if it did, it wasn't that big of a deal. In fact, it might have even left you disappointed.

Why not join me in doing a quick evaluation before you continue reading the rest of this chapter. What project are you currently spending a large part of your energy, time and money working on? Are you socking away money for an early retirement? Are you saving up and working two jobs to purchase a larger home? Has that vacation to an expensive location become a goal you are planning to reach and whatever sacrifice you need to make will be worth it? Are you continually dreaming about a luxury car that will someday be sitting in your driveway?

We all have dreams and goals, but at what expense will they be realized?

My focus in life began to change during our cancer journey and it was an important lesson I needed to learn. Our life was put on hold as far as material things were concerned. We did not have extra money and our future was so unknown, and I began to notice how much "future talk" is really part of so many people's lives. I realized that it had been dominant in my life as well.

Even now, at my age (mid-fifties), people are talking about winding down, planning ahead, and retiring. Prior to Pam's cancer experience I would have done the same. But not now. Like a magnet, the cancer journey pulled me relentlessly toward what's important.

What I noticed during the cancer journey was that I wanted to talk about something other than the future. Yet so many around me were continuing to acquire things and plan for the future, working so hard for something they would "someday" enjoy—while I was beginning to live only in the present.

The next time you're in a public place or with friends, pay attention to how much time people actually spend talking about the future. They are either complaining about something that is holding them back from their plans or they are working on a way to get something they want—a job, a house, a family, a raise, a trip. By nature, we live in the future. After cancer came, I noticed a switch in my conversation and, although I am visionary by nature, my life began to focus on what I had now.

I never regretted building that cabin, but it became less of a focal point in my life. There was a shift in terms of how much time, energy and money I was willing to invest in that ongoing project.

Have you ever noticed that when you're going through a very difficult situation in your life, people begin to respond differently toward you? Many people become kinder. Family members spend more time together. Communication increases. People become more empathetic and caring. Genuine efforts to see people in person become a priority. Prayers are more frequent. Hearts become more humble. Old friends begin to return. Conversations are more significant than before.

I have seen it over and over again in my years as a pastor and in my specific work with the sick and dying. Many people have indicated that this also happened in their life. I'm not saying this is a bad thing. In fact, quite the opposite. What I'm wondering is why does it have to wait until someone is sick, suffering or dying to happen?

What I noticed during Pam's cancer journey, I now try to carry over into my own life. It's a pretty sweet way to live. It came out of caring less about my cottage and caring more about the people I love and who love me. The following has become an unconscious mission statement for me.

- *I will intentionally choose to be kinder today.*
- *I will commit to spending time with my family today.*
- *I will check up on one friend today.*
- *I will pray for someone today.*
- *I will reach out and care, show empathy for someone outside my family.*
- *I will give thanks to God for all the ways that I've been blessed.*

CHAPTER 3
Tweaking the Way You Do Life

The values of the world we inhabit and the people we surround ourselves with have a profound effect on who we are.

— MALCOLM GLADWELL

I used to watch my grandpa adjust the carburetor on his 1965 blue Dodge. He was a mechanic. With a screwdriver in his right hand, he would turn the screw on the top of the carburetor ever so gently, from high to low, until the engine gave him that perfect purring sound he was after. "Now we can go for a drive," he'd say, often taking me out for a burger, fries and a Coke.

Have people ever told you that you have to make big changes in your life in order to begin to discover something new or different? I used to think that. What I noticed as we lived our lives from day to day in total uncertainty about our future, was that it was the small tweaks we made that helped us find that sweet spot. What is the sweet spot? It's when we are truly living out of our values.

People talk about their values a lot, whether they realize it or not. But taking time to examine them from time to time is not a common practice. Many of our values are formed early in life, and unless some significant event happens, we tend to hold on to those values from our childhood. Values are principles that guide and direct our decisions. Values are the compass of our ship. They give direction and allow us to navigate where we would like to go. In some cases, they also keep us from actually getting there.

Landon, our youngest son, brought home a baseball cap that was left on a field next to the playground. He was in second grade at the time. It was a cap that was very popular and had sold out in all the local stores. It was also over-priced because of its popularity. We asked him to take it back to where he had found it. He responded, "But someone else will find it and take it home!" "But perhaps the person who lost it will come back to look for it, too," I said to him. He returned the cap, a little reluctantly, but the principle that came from a value was embedded into Landon's life and is still evident today. It's called *integrity*: you do the right thing, even when no one is watching you.

Whether people believe it or not, we are all guided by our values. Taking a close look at them while you switch gears during a crisis is really important. Why? Because when you go through a crisis, you will find some changes happening in your life. A new perspective or a new way of living that is different for you than before may now come into conflict with others who are close to you. You've changed the rules on them. While our *personality* and the way we process information usually stay the same throughout our life (it's the bedrock of how we function), our *values* can change. You may change how you see and do life based upon a significant event occurring in your life. Living with cancer will do that.

Don't be surprised if there's a shift in what you once considered important as you begin to live with cancer. During the time of treatment and recovery, there will be plenty of time for reflecting and re-adjustments. The re-adjustment could be a small tweak or a cataclysmic shift.

In talking with many people who have gone through cancer, new questions emerge because of the uncertainty of their future. These are all questions that are connected with values. And the questions range from not only, "What if I die?" but also "What if I live? How will I live differently? Will the way that I engage and live my life in an ongoing way be any different than it was before this happened?"

I remember when a local resident, Jim, began to come to church following his daughter's death and his own battle with cancer. His wife did not understand that shift. Prior to these life-changing events, Jim rarely entered a church building. So what was happening? It was a change in one of his values. He wanted to pay more attention to God. He wanted to commit his time to understanding his spiritual life. The compass that was directing his ship was shifting. While his wife was surprised by his shift in priorities and his new way of understanding life, she respected him and honored this important readjustment in his life.

Have you ever been in a conversation with someone who has cancer and they begin to bargain? You hear them make promises to live life differently if they pull through. Have you done that yourself? Often people make promises to change the way they interact with others, God or their neighbor. I did. The person going through cancer and their family do not always recognize these changed values. As a result, they are often surprised by people's response to them, sometimes positive and sometimes negative. When people experience us and know us one way, they may be surprised when we make a significant shift in our values.

When you have cancer, you are forced to ask questions that lead to an evaluation of your values. And your family and friends who are looking on will also begin to ask questions about their own lives.

- Why am I here?
- Why do I exist?
- What is my role in this life?
- Why do I get up in the morning?
- Why do I do the work I do?
- What is my purpose right now?

Have you ever just stopped at the end of one day and said, "I need to make some changes in my life!"? It's because you know your values are not lining up with your behavior or the outcomes you desire. They are in competition with one another. A journey like cancer does a number on us and pushes us to consider deeper questions.

One of Pam's values was to work hard and do her best at whatever she was doing. She was a perfectionist and doing things to the very best of her ability was important to her. She would spend many late nights working on projects until she completed them and was satisfied with the results. She passed this work ethic on to her children as well. It became a part of who they were and was reflected in the sports award they often received: "Most Dedicated Player." This award was given to the hardest working player on the team.

Pam's work ethic came into play in her cancer journey as well, especially with her treatments and recovery times. She was courageous and worked hard, facing it head on. Nevertheless, because of her limited energy, she was forced to tweak that value and it became less a defining part of who she was as a person. Pam could no longer stay up late, and she began to make adjustments so other values in her life would not suffer. She only had so much time and energy available, so tweaking was important for Pam.

I quite liked the tweaks she made. She had more time for conversation; took opportunities to cuddle while watching a movie or television show (she had rarely watched movies); she began to read books for pleasure; and spent more time with family and friends without having to complete her tasks to perfection. While cancer treatments were a cruel master, they did afford her the chance to rest and spend more time with her family. Any perfectionism was given a backseat.

I know my life began to change as a result of living with a wife who had cancer. More than anything, the values I espoused began to be lived out more intentionally. Those things I deemed to be important values in my life began to be more evident in my behavior. I suppose I began walking the talk more consistently. The values of strong family, a vibrant faith, and a close community of good friends started to show up even more powerfully. The way I responded, acted, and prioritized my time, energy and resources began to line up with my values. These were necessary tweaks that in hindsight I'm grateful for.

As a result of Pam's deeper questions at a crossroads in her life, I, too, began to ask a set of questions. They helped me to shape and organize my life differently because of what I noticed during our cancer journey. These are questions you may want to consider in the midst of your cancer journey as well:

- What's most important to me and why? Are there any shifts happening to what I value?
- How do I want to live life? Have I made any recognizable adjustments that are important?
- How do I want to be treated? Have I changed my perception of how I want people to engage me?
- How will I treat others? Am I interacting with others differently than before?
- How do I make decisions? Am I looking at my daily decisions from a new perspective?
- What do I really believe? Am I showing people around me something new about myself?

When our behavior matches our values, then our lives generally bring us joy. We are fulfilled and satisfied. When we experience unhappiness, it is usually the result of misaligned values. It is then that we begin to struggle with life. Of course you are going to struggle and experience times of sadness and uncertainty. That's part of life.

The truth is, our emotions will be at a peak because of this roller coaster ride we are on. Because emotions are linked to our values, they become a measuring stick of how we are doing. Understanding our emotions is key because they are linked to our values. We need all the help we can get during this journey, so why not recognize the place of values and their importance in our ongoing life?

Emotions such as joy, confidence, a sense of fulfillment and meaningfulness can be the result of living according to our core values—we are on course and headed where we want to go. Anxiety, anger, or guilt may warn us that a value is being violated, threatened or overlooked in our lives. Our 'gut' tells us when we are experiencing inner dissonance due to a behavior-values incongruity.

Bottom line, a changing emotion lets you know there's been a shift, something isn't jiving for you. Having a conversation around that value may be necessary in order to maintain healthy relationships as you continue your journey.

Because values ultimately shape:

- The way you behave
- How you communicate
- What is important to you
- Where you spend your money and time
- How you make choices

Your family and friends should recognize what is important to you and encourage you to live out of our values, even though yours may differ from theirs and may have even changed as a result of what you are currently experiencing.

Make sense? Make small tweaks to the carburetor, if necessary, and then the engine can purr!

CHAPTER 4
Finding Your Purpose When You Can't Move

There is more to life than increasing its speed.
— MAHATMA GANDHI

You would think a stage-three ovarian cancer diagnosis would keep you down. But nine months after Pam finished her first round of chemo treatments and the ensuing recovery period, she went back to substitute teaching. She returned before her hair grew back and had some amazing conversations with the school kids she loved so much. She was a mom but she was also a natural teacher. She taught Brownies, led children's choirs and loved to be involved with children who were struggling with English. She knew her purpose and continued to walk in it.

Our children seemed to adjust well. Devon, our oldest, went off to university. The other three teenagers (grades 8, 10 and 12) settled into another year of school. We continued to live as we had before, with crazy athletic schedules and heavy school activities.

And then there was me...

I started to question *my* purpose and *my* vocation. I know it might sound crazy, but Pam's cancer journey shook *me* up like a dog shakes a well-worn toy in its mouth. I couldn't make decisions quickly because I had to readjust and make sure I was taking care of my wife and family the best I could. I realized I was being cracked open so new insights could find their way into my life.

Prior to Pam's cancer diagnosis, I used to make my life happen like I wanted it to. I knew where I needed to go and was quite successful in most areas of my life.

But now I had given up my international clientele because I couldn't travel with Pam sick at home. I began to close down part of my company. And I took a position at a local company in sales and marketing.

- Have circumstances ever restricted you from fulfilling your plans?
- Have finances ever stopped you from moving forward?
- Has a downturn in the market ever squeezed you out of a job?
- Has your own health ever forced you to stop working for a period of time?
- Has a sick or troubled family member ever forced you to re-evaluate steps you were planning to take?
- Are your aging parents in need of your attention?

I became very frustrated because of the interruptions in my life, believing that somehow I was not really moving forward in any recognizable manner. But then I came to the place where I realized there was something deeper happening. So I said to myself, *Why not look beneath the soil? See if there is a seed that is growing beneath that hard dirt that has formed, waiting to surprise you with something new.* So I dug beneath the hard soil and was surprised by what I discovered.

Many men have said to me that they feel very helpless when their wife, child or family member develops cancer. The phrase "I can't fix this" is very common. I know I certainly said it. I was able to fix almost anything in my life—but not this.

My big "aha" moment came when I realized that *I* was the one needing to be fixed. Mark Twain once said, "The two most important days in your life are the day you were born and the day you find out why." Nobody chooses to go through difficult challenges, but I have to admit that my life changed forever because of my journey with Pam. As we began to move into a new way of living, my purpose started to stir within me.

I have spent hours with people as a counselor and pastor talking about their purpose. People always want to know if there is a bigger plan for them—if they were made for a greater purpose. Call it unrest, unhappiness or just genuine curiosity, but just about everyone comes to that question eventually: "Is this all there is for me?"

God called me to be a pastor—very clearly. Pretty nearly banged me over the head and, believe you me, I fought it tooth and nail. The ministry was the last place I wanted to be, for a variety of reasons. I went to university primarily to play hockey and meet girls—no career path in mind except being a goalie for an NHL team. I planned to enjoy my college years and play hockey at the same time. It would be fun!

During my second year I met a girl (not my future wife) who was a Christian and who helped me explore faith and asked me some deep questions—not related to hockey. The third year I met another Christian girl who encouraged me to look at ministry and asked if God was calling me to be a pastor. "No way!" was my answer to her. I loved sports and thought that Recreation Administration would be a good fit for me. Besides, I didn't fit in with the pre-theology students who attended chapel and Bible studies on campus. I played hockey, drank beer and dated girls. I had faith, but it didn't seem to be lived out the same way as the others around me who were preparing "seriously" for the ministry. From my perspective, I thought I would be a terrible pastor.

Barb, the girl I dated in my third year, had a gift. Reader beware, you may find this next part a little weird.

Early one morning, I was awakened by a phone call from Barb. I assumed something was wrong because of the tone of her voice. "You have to come over here quickly. I need to talk to you!" she said. So I put my clothes on and ran to the other side of the campus. As I arrived, she hugged me and cried. "What's wrong?" I asked. "Nothing," she said. "Here, this is for you," she said, handing me a folded piece of paper. "What is it?" I asked. "It's a letter—a letter from God. I woke up from my sleep and I heard God's voice telling me to write these words down. So I did. What He said is in this letter."

I sat there in shock for a few moments. *Was this real? Does this kind of stuff really happen? Why would God want to speak to me in this extraordinary and strange way?* The letter was addressed to me, "My dear child, Rick…" I read the letter and began to weep. I had never read a more beautifully poetic letter in my life. It was beyond what any human could pen—way beyond what I had ever heard Barb say or write. In the letter, God was telling me that I was to become a *shepherd*, a pastor.

You would think that after this letter it would be a no-brainer, but I still struggled with accepting the call to be a pastor. In the end, however, I did give in to my purpose.

I became a pastor six years later, served in a church for ten years, and then I quit. I left the church, partly out of my insecurity and partly because of some seemingly insurmountable challenges. But I think it was also because I needed to learn some things about life and obtain some skills from the secular world.

I worked as a marketing director and soon found myself loving this next phase of my life outside the church. I formed my own company. I was successful. I had a great run. I was doing very well. All was progressing as planned and then… bang! CANCER. My plans were turned upside down and I began to question my purpose and vocation once again.

Only six months following Pam's cancer diagnosis, I began to wonder what my future would hold. I was being pulled back into my original purpose and calling, even though I didn't realize it at first. I didn't want to consider it, but Pam's encouragement in the midst of her cancer journey helped me return to full-time ministry.

Initially I resented having to jump through the hoops of taking extended courses in order to comply with church policy. In the midst of caring for Pam, it meant being away for three months in order to take a hospital chaplaincy course. At least it was in the summer and Pam was out at the lake enjoying the kids and the fresh outdoors. So I traveled back and forth fulfilling my responsibilities.

My time at the hospital in an extended chaplaincy course was good. It seemed to me that taking the training, with a wife who had gone through cancer and a family that was transitioning, provided further empathy and insights which were honed in my work with people at the hospital.

Then the call came from a church in the town of Cochrane, just outside of Calgary, Alberta. I was not looking for the call. It was totally unexpected. I was offered a pastor position by this church that was ideal for me. Let me rephrase that—ideal *for us* and more specifically for Pam.

I found it fascinating that even though my wife was confident in her purpose and vocation, heading back to school and teaching, continuing her work and role in the community, being an awesome mom—all this following her cancer treatments—I was the one to question my vocation. And it centered on the question of purpose.

When do you ask questions about your purpose? When things are going well or when you are restless?

When do you contemplate something different in your life? When you are content or when you are in transition?

When things are in turmoil or uncertain, when plans are not going as hoped, that's the time to sit down and listen to what needs to be spoken. It's hard to catch up to a speeding vehicle. I had been on fast-forward most of my life. It was now time to turn over the soil and look for the new growth underneath.

I found my purpose again when I could not be on the move and do what I wanted to, when I had time to listen carefully to my heart, people and God.

I actually went on a walk by myself to reflect and contemplate for the first time in my life. In the past, I would have considered it a waste of time because I wasn't accomplishing anything. I needed help discovering what was next for me and I found it in the most unlikely place: Pam's cancer journey. I was finally taking notice of what was happening inside of *me*.

I was a butterfly emerging from a chrysalis, needing to strengthen my own wings. I couldn't remain a caterpillar this time — I had to emerge from this dark cocoon and fly.

I had found my wings! Again!

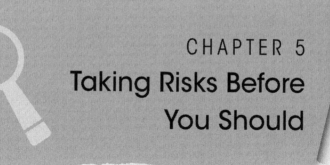

CHAPTER 5
Taking Risks Before
You Should

*A ship is always safe at the shore—but
that is NOT what it is built for.*
— ALBERT EINSTEIN

There are some days when our lives feel like a bunch of tangled knots on a long fishing pole. There are just too many decisions to make and too much going on. Life has a grip on us and we don't know what to do.

We try to settle into our lives but unexpected things happen and another knot is added to the line. It takes a lot of energy to untangle knots, until you realize that each time you untangle a knot it brings you closer to your goal.

That used to happen to me when I'd go fishing as a kid. I'm not sure how I did it, but I managed to tangle up my line so much I couldn't cast anymore. "Dad! Please help me untangle my line!" I would ask. "You can do it, Rick. Just be patient—one knot at a time," he would tell me calmly as he watched me work away at it. Sometimes he would even step in at the last moment when the knot was at its tightest and help me undo it.

What a feeling to finally be able to cast again. And it was an even better feeling when I caught a big fish on the end of that line.

Living with cancer is like living in the middle of a huge, tangled knot. There are so many unknowns piled up on top of each other. And then you settle in and begin to untangle the knots. What I didn't realize was that I had other knots needing to be untangled that would set me free once I was rid of them. And Pam helped me to untangle the last one.

I'd taken some risks in life before, but usually I had a backup plan to ensure my stability. Or at least something to protect me from potential bankruptcy. So perhaps that's not really risk-taking. Up until then, the biggest risk I had taken was leaving my full-time job in the ministry. And at that time I was pretty sure that with my skill set, work ethic, support of family and God's provision, I would be okay to take the next step. Some people thought I was crazy. We had four children, aged six, five, three and one, and Pam was a stay-at-home mom. I quit my church job on a Sunday and got a job in sales the next day. It added a whole new dimension to my life and what I loved to do. I had not put anything into place. It just fell into my lap.

If you're a person who needs to put everything in order before stepping out, you may never discover what's next and you may miss out on incredible opportunities. I learned this principle even more as I watched how Pam was interacting with us as a family, with her friends and with her community during her cancer journey—during a time when she was having the stuffing knocked out of her.

It was during this time period, two years into her cancer journey, that I took my next big risk and this time nothing made sense about it at all. If I had tried to make sense of the step, I never would have taken it in the first place and I would have missed out on some amazing events and new relationships that impacted my life greatly.

Have you ever read the Bible story about Jesus walking on water? His disciples are in a boat rowing for their lives because of the heavy winds. Then Jesus starts walking toward them on the water. Are they glad to see Him? No! They're terrified. They think He's a ghost. Then Peter, one of the guys in the boat, decides he wants to do the same thing. Big risk, considering he isn't wearing a life jacket and he's in the middle of a windstorm. But Jesus likes the idea and invites Peter to join him. Everything's good until Peter realizes how big the waves really are and that he can't swim in this kind of storm. He takes his eyes off Jesus to review his situation and starts to sink. Jesus holds out his hand, grabs him and saves him.

I love this story. Peter is so ready to take a risk, even without being sure of the outcome. It's only when he begins to fear that he starts to sink — but it does turn out fine for Peter. In fact, this act of faith allowed Peter to become stronger. His choleric personality made him impetuous and rash at times, but it was honed and used for good and Peter became Jesus's main man later on. In fact, Jesus called him "the rock."

Why do I tell this story? Because I've noticed over the years in my professional life that some individuals totally put their life on hold once they are diagnosed: no dreams, no hopes, no initiatives, no vision. Some of these individuals even want those around them to put their lives on hold as well, asking their families to give up on dreams and future plans. And some family members opt for that in the fray of uncertainty: *Stay in the boat. Don't move. You don't know how to swim. You can't walk on water. No risks, please. Just wait until I'm finished working through this challenge.*

When Pam got sick, I immediately began to downshift my gears and focus on her, because I felt it was the right thing to do. She needed to be the focus, right? But Pam would have nothing to do with that attitude! She would not allow me or the children to be held back in our lives. Her life was on hold for a time, but she was adamant that *our* lives wouldn't be. It was almost as if she gained a voice of authority in this matter because she couldn't look too far ahead herself. It seemed to me that she knew the importance of each of us fulfilling our God-given purpose and wasn't afraid to allow us to step out into that. This is a very important lesson. I needed to learn it for that time and today I still use it in my own life.

Here are the potential responses if that person dies or if that person regains their health: a) "I feel so guilty that I did not spend enough time with that person before they died," or b) "I'm angry that they held me back for so long because of unrealistic expectations that they placed on my life." Both are normal, but neither is necessary.

Have you ever noticed when you are going through a tough time that others are reluctant to share their good news with you? They don't want you to feel bad. I've done that – downplayed the good stuff in my life so that others wouldn't feel worse. I would stop short of letting people know all the meaningful and good things that were going on in my life. In fact, I tended not to want to share anything about my future plans because, deep down, I wondered if they had any plans of their own. But then I noticed how Pam handled other people's good news and a light went on for me. She knew how to celebrate with people's good stuff even in the midst of her bad stuff.

I was around many people who were struggling with cancer at the same time Pam was. As they came away from their treatment, cancer free, Pam would be the first one to send them a card, phone them or celebrate their victory. I sat back and marveled. She was infectious. Sometimes I wanted to say, "Come on, God, why not Pam? Isn't it our turn for some good news? When will our circumstances change?"

I learned a very valuable lesson from this tiny wife of mine. So I began to choose to celebrate with others who were now free from this disease. I was thankful they had a brighter future and a new beginning. They were stepping out into something new. It was hope realized again! Hope for them and hope for us, too.

There is something extremely powerful that happens when a person who is suffering, hurting or dying chooses to challenge, encourage and empower those around them to step out into their dream. It makes you want to realize your purpose all the more. Then it hit me. *Instead of waiting until the end of our lives to encourage people to become bigger, why don't we do it now, every day?*

As a result, I decided to engage in people's life in a positive and encouraging way, even if I wasn't feeling overly effervescent on a given day. I learned to invite people to share their successes and their stories, regardless of my emotions or current circumstances. I realized it actually began to change my heart. It did not leave me envious or jealous as I thought it would. Instead, I felt hopeful. I began to see how life does change. That God is moving in people's lives. Great things are happening despite life having its challenges. There is hope, just watch for it.

Pam held none of us back. We took big risks when maybe others wouldn't have—all because of her attitude of celebration and ability to encourage others to get into life and work it for all its beauty and wonder.

Our next risk—our move to the new church in Cochrane—was a big risk for all of us. We were leaving a community where we had lived and raised our children for 15 years. It was home for them. Keeara was in her last year of high school. Devon was going off to University for another term. Larissa was moving into grade 11 and Landon into grade 9. This move meant a new community, a new school and new friends for these young people. That's a lot of transition for such young lives!

Pam was managing the best she could. She had a very good oncologist. We had a wonderful community to support us during this time. It would have been easier to stay put in the familiar. But Pam would not hold me back and was willing to take the risk to move on. I am still amazed at our move, when it made no logical sense at all.

So we packed up and left town to experience a new adventure in the midst of an ongoing cancer journey. Some of you may say, "How could you do that? It was unfair to Pam and your kids!" But it was for the best in the end and Pam actually received better care as a result. But we didn't know that when we moved.

That was August 2005, two years following her initial diagnosis. It was taking a risk before we should have, but it became one of the best decisions we ever made.

- Is anything holding you back from moving into the next important step in your life?
- Do you need to move out of your current circumstances even though it doesn't appear to make sense?
- Is something inside you saying, "Yes, now is the time!"?
- Is there a right time to make a move?

Yes, life can tangle us up in knots. It may be time to untangle what's holding you back and discover the next adventure.

Fishing anyone?

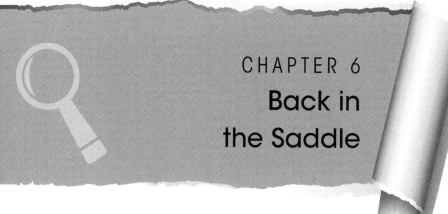

CHAPTER 6

Back in the Saddle

It's not how hard you hit. It's how hard you get hit...and keep moving forward.
— RANDY PAUSCH

"**G**et back on that horse!" he hollered. A group of us guys had gone away for the weekend, and part of our experience was to be involved in a small cattle drive. But one man's horse got startled and bucked him off. Not hard, but just enough for him to say, "I'm not getting back on that horse! I'll walk back to the ranch!" "Get back on the horse!" our leader insisted. "No!" he protested. "You get back on that horse, Mister!" he said emphatically and began to swagger toward the petulant, would-be cowboy. He finally did get back in the saddle and the rest of the cattle drive went smoothly.

It's important to know that multiple losses are part of a cancer journey. These are known as *concurrent losses*. We need to be prepared to get back in the saddle regardless of the setbacks that accompany this journey. We must not stay down or allow these losses to keep us in a place of despair. Hope is a much-needed characteristic when you are in transitional loss.

In December of 2005, we headed to Edmonton for some possible answers to Pam's cancer. The doctor was surprised by Pam's cancer because there was no pre-disposition that made any sense: no life-style issues, no past physical problems, no family history, no lack of exercise or healthy eating, not even age group issues. They wanted to do some genetic testing, and we agreed. We were hoping to find out some news, good or bad. It would be important for our kids to be aware of possible health issues in their future.

It turned out to be an important meeting, but the day included a second unexpected loss. We were hit twice in one day.

We had moved to Cochrane before selling our home in Westlock, four hours away. We had to leave the old house in the hands of the real estate agent to maintain and hopefully sell. As I sat in the waiting room of the genetic clinic waiting for Pam to come out of her appointment, I received a phone call.

"Rick?" I heard the real estate agent's voice on the other end of the line. "We have a problem with your house," he said. "What? What kind of problem?" I asked. "A water line broke and it's been running for a few days. Your house is flooded. We shut off the water but it's a big mess." I detected a note of anxiety in his voice and rightly so.

We were only one hour away at that point, so I knew we would have to get up there quickly once Pam was done at the doctor's. In the meantime, I needed to focus on her. That was not an easy thing to do.

Pam came out into the waiting room. I didn't say anything to her. "We can go now," she said. "Okay, Honey. Did you get the results?" I asked. "Yes," she said. "Stop for a moment," I said to her. "Look at me." Pam looked up and said, "I have a genetic defect that is called BRCA 1 or 2. That's the reason for the cancer." "Why was this not evident in any of your family of origin?" I asked. "I don't know," she shrugged, "but at least we know now." "Well, it's a little late for you," I replied, showing a touch of anger, probably because my mind was also dealing with the potential disaster at our old home. "Rick," Pam continued, "this is important information for our girls to know." Pam always found the good in everything.

I hesitated to tell her about the phone call that I had received in the waiting room. We had a lot of equity tied up in the old house that we planned to use to eventually purchase a new home in Cochrane, a very pricey part of Alberta.

I got up my courage, "Pam, I got a phone call from the real estate agent while I was in the waiting room. A water line broke in our Westlock home. There's some water damage. If it's okay with you, I'd like to drive there and assess the damage." "How could that have happened?" she asked. "I don't know, but we need to deal with it." "Well, it's fortunate that we're so close," she said, and we drove up that afternoon.

We loved our little house. Pam had made it a home and we had raised our four children there. I can still visualize waking up in the wee hours of the morning and peeking bleary-eyed into the living room where, in the white rocking chair, Pam sat rocking and singing her newest baby, Landon, back to sleep. Or getting up for a glass of water and seeing Pam working away at the kitchen table late at night, helping the kids with their science projects, or writing a note to place in their lunch bags.

As we drove, we talked about the genetic information she had just been given. It was a short conversation. For Pam, if you have no control over something, there is no sense in complaining about it, focusing on it or even discussing it. And so the conversation turned toward our children, her sisters and her nieces. "We need to let them know right away so they can get tested, and also maybe the cousins as well," Pam continued the conversation as we drove down the highway.

We walked in the front door of our home and were shocked by the damage. The fitting on the dishwasher had apparently given out, they told us, and the water had been running for nearly three days, non-stop. The basement was completely flooded; water had run down the walls and the ceiling was destroyed. The rugs were unsalvageable. Even most of the main floor had water damage of some significance. Pam wept. I held her close.

I knew that she was not crying for the house, but for all the hard work that we had put into getting it ready to sell. She was also weeping for the deep memories attached to that place. I wondered if it was fair that we had been dealt yet another blow. "It's going to be okay," I assured her. "We will make it," but secretly I wondered in my heart why we were being thrown another curve ball, especially two in one day.

As I thought things through, my conversation with God soon took on a different tone. I began to shout out to the Almighty, "I don't care about this house, God! You can have it, but please don't take away my wife and the mother of my children! Please!"

This would not be the last challenge we would face in this time period.

A week later we received the full report from the genetics clinic recommending Pam have a double mastectomy as soon as possible. The risk of breast cancer was now higher because of her ovarian cancer and it was important to be proactive. Without hesitation, she phoned the doctor to arrange for the earliest possible mastectomy. She got back on her horse and kept riding, but I wondered how much more this girl could take.

Pam spoke with a friend who had had a mastectomy and asked about her experience. Pam hid nothing. She wanted people at the church to pray for her. This open honesty and confidence permeated our family's life and invited others to experience the transition with us in what we hoped was a healthy way.

Pam was an unbelievable woman who was confident in who she was and not dependent upon two pieces of flesh to define her significance. Not that I wouldn't miss those body parts as her husband, but this was about her, not me. I loved her and honored her decision because I wanted her to live. So she was scheduled for yet another operation.

Multiple losses—our home was flooded and we lost all of our equity in it, Pam had both breasts removed, and my Dad was dying from terminal cancer. "Enough is enough!" I thought. Then, almost immediately following Pam's mastectomy, the doctors found more cancer—it had returned. The chemo treatments began all over again. And all she could say was, "Well let's get going then." She was one tough and courageous lady—much braver than I.

The cancer journey is more than enough to handle without everyday life issues. But we live in a world where bad things do happen and they don't always come upon us in a gentlemanly fashion. They sometimes come all at once, like an ambush. So where do you get your strength to get back in the saddle when multiple losses occur?

- Your parent gets sick.
- You lose your job.
- Your child is being bullied at school.
- Finances become very tight.
- Your child moves back home with her baby.
- A good friend leaves your community.
- A relative gets divorced.
- Your child dies.
- You have a miscarriage.
- Your home burns down.
- You are terminally ill.

It's not easy to experience loss, especially one after another. Each loss will knock you down and endeavor to keep you there. I was amazed at how Pam was able to get back on her horse, even though it kept bucking her off time and again.

Why do bad things seem to happen to good people? Actually bad things happen to *everybody* because we live in a broken world. No one is exempt from unexpected challenges. We may have brought the hard knocks on ourselves and may be living in misery as a result of our own choices. Or we may have had nothing to do with the trauma we're experiencing. Either way, troubles come. I'm not being pessimistic, just realistic.

As I meet with people in my counseling practice and seek to determine why they are depressed or experiencing sadness, so often it comes down to multiples losses that have been left unexamined and are compounded into one big, heavy load. Often these people have not been mentored or parented in "good" transition. We learn transition from our family of origin and through our ongoing experiences with other significant people. If we have not learned how to transition well by observing it in others, then adapting in times of crisis or loss becomes almost impossible.

Oddly enough, one of the benefits of living in my family of origin was that we moved a lot. It was hard sometimes, but it provided a framework for me to learn about how to transition through a loss and find joy on the other side. I did not want to have to leave my friends, try out for another hockey team, attend another school or move to another neighborhood. All of these were losses. Sometimes I just wished we could have stayed put in one place long enough for me to call it "home." But in hindsight, I discovered that "home" went beyond our four walls to where my family was together. Mom and Dad taught us about transition very effectively. They also gave us the freedom to fall and get back up on our own as well.

Most of my counseling work is in helping people with transition. I have noticed that rather than help, empower, and teach children about transition, today's parents would rather protect them from a world that is not always safe, fair or happy. Of course, we want to take care of our children and they need to know they are safe, but we need to provide tools for them at home as they grow, preparing them to step out into the real world. We will be bucked off the horse many times in our lives. If we don't learn how to get back on, can we expect anything different in how we will respond or react to challenges when they come our way as we get older?

Using the horse analogy, why not try these steps the next time you hit the dirt:

- Get back in the saddle again—you can't ride if you aren't on the horse.
- Give it a kick and go for another ride—it might take you somewhere different this time.
- Take the reins and give it some direction—it might go where you need it to go.
- Take a new trail you have never been on before—it might lead to new adventures.
- Choose to let it walk, trot, or run. Choose your own pace, but choose to move forward.
- Let the wind blow your hair back and enjoy the ride.

"Get back on that horse!" the guy said.

Pam did that over and over again. I'd like to think that I can get back in the saddle, too. And so can you.

CHAPTER 7
Information Overload: Learning How to Filter

Too much information running through my brain.
Too much information driving me insane.
— THE POLICE

t was back. The remission was short-lived. Pam started her second round of treatments in February 2006.

Everyone had been so hopeful. Pam had done so well. Her hair had even grown back. She now had curly blonde hair instead of straight hair. She was beautiful. I was proud of her but knew she would have to emotionally adjust to going through it all over again. We all would.

Chemotherapy is not fun. Ingesting chemicals into your body to kill bad cells also kills some of the good things your body needs. But this was our only option, so we had to continue to believe and trust that we were doing everything possible to get rid of this disease.

A few times Pam became very dehydrated. Once I even took her to the hospital so she could get some electrolytes back into her system. The body is so complex and every organ works with the others in a mysterious way.

I bought a nice glass water carafe and set it on her nightstand so she could always have water available to cleanse her system and hydrate her body. "This is so good!" she would say, drinking as much of the purified water as she could handle following her treatments.

You learn quickly about your body when you are on a cancer journey. You discover what's beneficial and what's not. We bought a juicer, vitamins, and special teas. We went to a naturopath physician. We completely changed our diet, eliminating foods that were not helpful. I had a stack of heath books related to cancer. As a family, we began to change what we took into our bodies and that was a good decision.

We learned another important lesson when we began to experience a huge volume of information coming into our lives regarding "tried and true" cures for cancer. The overload had an impact upon our health and happiness. I realized that I needed to come up with a strategy for filtering the information before jumping headlong into the latest fad or cancer cure.

Have you ever been in a situation where you decided to believe a piece of erroneous information and paid the consequences for it later? You said to yourself, "Why didn't I think about that first before buying in? Why didn't I research that better?"

For me, it was not so much about asking for advice, which is important, too, but it was learning to discern the information I was reading in books or online, watching in documentaries or hearing from concerned friends who wanted to help. Sometimes too much information is hard to handle. If you don't filter it first, you end up spinning your wheels, running out of resources and becoming discouraged.

I recently counseled a young woman who asked me to come to the hospital where she had been admitted. The medical team was preparing her for some aggressive chemotherapy. It was breast cancer. The tests had indicated a quick spread of the cancer and the decision was to not delay the treatment. She was frightened, scared and confused.

After spending some time with her, we concluded that her unrest came from the differing opinions about her situation. One person would cite a fact based on their experience, while another source would say the opposite. She was trying to maintain a hopeful attitude, but the hope she found quickly disappeared with each piece of new information. Sometimes going to the Internet for information can exacerbate the situation — and this was true in her case. The more she read, the more fearful she became. I suggested that, for the time being, she not go online for any further information. I also suggested that she closely monitor how she received information from family, friends and acquaintances, so that she could guard her heart.

Have you ever become obsessed by a concern in your life, started searching for solutions and become more anxious as a result? You reach out and ask others who are close to you for input, but are still left without suitable answers. Your angst then brings you to known experts who deal with that specific issue — and still you find no peace of mind. You are left more confused, trying to manage the differing opinions and tidbits of information as if they were numerous corks being held under water.

If you have read my previous book, *Finding Anchors*, you will know that sometimes our personality differences impact the way in which we prefer to process the information that is presented to us. Some people are geared toward wanting more details — they need it in order to organize their lives. They don't like loose ends. Unfortunately, with cancer there are always loose ends. With thousands of differing medical, psychological and biological studies, the one who continues to look for conclusive information on a cancer prognosis is in for a difficult ride, unless a boundary around the incoming arsenal of information is in place.

I know that we certainly felt bombarded with information—much of it not applicable to Pam's situation. It seemed like every time I would run into a person in the community, they would have an opinion on what they thought we should be considering. Sometimes it was based on their life or a friend's experience or a book they had read—everything from *pau d'arco* tea to juicing to famous naturopaths who could cure people's cancer in a week or two.

It became overwhelming as we tried to manage our lives and come to a place where we were comfortable with how things were progressing and the decisions we had made. That wasn't an easy place to find. It was a strange phenomenon, but the second round of chemotherapy brought forth even more suggestions from people. It's as if people were becoming desperate for Pam and our family.

Has that ever happened to you? It's not that people were unkind—it's that people were speaking from *their* experience and point of view. It may not apply to us. Or it may be spoken out of their need to contribute in some way. It becomes a way for people to cope and not have to deal with the unknowns of the situation. They're trying to control the uncontrollable.

Even as I write this book, I present it only from my own personal life and from my professional experience and how I have integrated this information. I'm well aware that not everyone who reads this book will follow it to the letter and not every word will resonate with each person—and that's okay. I want you to filter this information *also* and decide what makes sense for you and what does not. There is not a cookie cutter approach to living with cancer.

I have spent a lot of my time counseling people, helping them undo damage caused by misguided and inaccurate information. You cannot just accept or welcome everything that comes into your life without good discernment. Just because someone says it, doesn't mean it's true. And paper doesn't refuse ink.

Here are a few examples from my counseling experience. I'm certain that you could add your own to the list:

- a financial expert gives us bad advice on an investment and it fails
- a co-worker suggests a blind date and it's a disaster
- a neighbor suggests how to approach a disgruntled family member and it turns out worse
- an acquaintance tells us about a miracle herb that costs us thousands of dollars and then makes no difference
- a doctor recommends an experimental drug and we get sicker
- Here are some questions you might consider asking if you feel overloaded by information:
- Who is the source of the information? Do you know them personally?
- Have you spoken to another person who has used this information? More than one person?
- Does it come from a person of wisdom and credibility? Not only professionals, but people with experience?
- Do you have any immediate red flags about the source of this information? Write them down.
- Are you having trouble sleeping at night? It's an indicator of unrest within you.
- How is your mental state? Are you more confused than before?
- Do you feel anxious about the information? An anxious mind and heart are saying something to you.
- Are you questioning its benefits or promises? Your gut feeling is important to consider.
- Is there conflict between family members or others about this information? Listen carefully to others who have your best interest in mind.

- Is the information you took into your life causing you to make bad decisions? Maybe you need to reconsider.
- How are you responding to those closest to you? Are your relationships changing? Ask why.

Most people with whom I speak who are dealing with cancer are searching for options and solutions to their disease. That's fair. You will tend to give people your ear because you want to be totally rid of this disease and want to consider all the options.

Here's a great idea. Find a good friend to be your information buffer. Ask them to do the research for you and bring back the results. You need to heal. You need to rest. You need to have a heart free from this stress and the information that overloads you.

Learning to filter is just plain smart!

CHAPTER 8

Letting Go of What Is Good

Some people believe holding on and hanging in there are signs of great strength. However, there are times when it takes much more strength to know when to let go and then do it.

— ANN LANDERS

My Dad was in an extended care facility at the same time that Pam was going through cancer treatments. I felt pulled in two directions. I knew that my father's cancer was terminal and that his time on earth was coming to an end and yet I also had a wife who was in the midst of finishing her treatments and would need my ongoing support. I was torn.

The angst that I felt was intense as I thought about my dad, lying in bed three hours away. I did my best to visit him, but it never seemed to be enough for me. I remember clearly driving up to see him on a day off. We chatted for a while and then I needed to say what was really on my heart. "Dad, I'm really sorry that I can't be here more often. I feel so bad," I said and began to cry. He looked at me, and taking both my hands in his, he said, "Rick, your priority is your wife. Pam needs you. It's okay. We had our life together. It was good. We will see each other again. But right now you need to spend time with your wife and your family." We both shed more tears – and then we hugged each other.

Letting go of what's good. That was hard for me and yet my father released me in a beautiful and empowering way.

When we first moved to Cochrane and waited for our home to sell back in Westlock, we lived at Pam's uncle and aunt's farm just outside of Calgary. Three of our four children lived with us. I was so happy to have them in our home, especially during this time when their mom was ill. I thought it was the perfect situation. Our oldest was away at university, but the rest of the family was together.

It was there that I discovered the importance of letting go of what I considered to be good — or at least good for me, but not necessarily good for others. I should have learned this from my dad, but it was actually my wife who taught me the importance of the principle of letting go.

Keeara, our oldest daughter decided to go on a mission trip to an orphanage in Haiti. I was not sure about this idea because Pam still had cancer. I did not want Keeara away from us. But Pam said, "She needs to go."

Larissa had attended grade 11 in Cochrane, but she really missed her friends back in Westlock and wanted to graduate in the community in which she had grown up. Finishing her final year of high school in Westlock would mean a year away from us. I was uncomfortable with it since Pam was still struggling with cancer and I didn't want Larissa to leave her mom. But once again Pam said, "She needs to go."

This was not the first time Pam was able to let go of her children. Devon went off to university the September following Pam's diagnosis. I thought Devon should stay home for a year and work. But Pam said, "He needs to go."

Landon was asked to play triple A hockey the same summer Pam was going through her treatments and I thought Landon should stay with Pam as the other kids had summer jobs. But Pam said, "He needs to go."

These conversations that I had with Pam taught me a valuable lesson: what *we* want isn't necessarily good for others. Life is really all about letting go. We are not called to hold on to people, but to release them to move forward in growth.

I had always been amazed at how empowering Pam was with all of our children. It seems I was living more in fear of the unknown than she was.

And then we had to sell our cabin. That was one of the most difficult decisions I had to make, considering the time and effort I had personally put into that cabin. We spent the last summer together fixing it up for resale. Every day I struggled with the reality of letting go of that piece of paradise and every day I grieved the day we would drive away from the cottage for the very last time.

I also did not want to leave the apple tree we had planted in the front yard. The tree was in memory of my dear Grandma. She was a rock in our family. She had planted it with my mom a few years earlier, before Grandma died. It took a few years before it bloomed and produced apples, but now it was strong and we harvested a lot of apples every year.

Life really is a series of "letting go" experiences. And if we don't let go, we may never see the fruit that might bloom as a result of our decision.

- Devon became a Computer Engineer.
- Keeara returned from the Haiti orphanage and, because of her experience there, became a teacher.
- Larissa is in her final year of Law School.

- Landon is an entrepreneur.
- We bought a beautiful home in Cochrane.
- And my Dad died.

I am still learning to let go of things in my life, but I learned so much by taking notice of how Pam was able to release people, possessions and goals. Hopefully this will continue to bear fruit in my future.

Is there anything in your life that you need to let go of?

Are you holding back someone in your life and not allowing them to produce fruit?

CHAPTER 9
Plugging Into Something Deeper

You cannot truly listen to anyone and do anything else at the same time.
— M. SCOTT PECK

I get a buildup of wax in my ears that needs to be cleaned out every six months or so. It becomes too thick and it doesn't matter what I do, I finally end up going to the doctor. It feels gross while the doctor is spraying water into my ear, but oh so good afterwards! Ironically, I have noticed that when my ears are plugged, I actually listen more attentively because I don't want to miss out on what's being said. I lean into the conversation, looking directly at the person and read their lips in order to get the full meaning of what they're saying.

Steven Covey, in his book *The 7 Habits of Highly Effective People*, suggests a very important principle: "Seek first to understand, and then to be understood."[1] How many people do you know who practice this principle? Do you practice it?

Replay a one-on-one conversation you had recently. It could have been with a spouse, partner, co-worker, child, neighbor or friend. What percentage of the conversation was you listening to them? It's often humbling to examine how we listen and to discover how poor our listening skills really are. And, by the way, just because you did not say anything, does not mean you are a good listener. You could have been off in your own world, in your own thoughts, while someone poured their heart out to you.

We can be physically present but emotionally and attentively absent. Neither approach to listening captures what might be hidden behind the words. In either case, you miss out on the important conversation that needs to take place that tells a deeper story. When we do all the talking, we interfere with someone else's story and actually don't connect with them at all.

Every day I hear people in the coffee shop, fitness club and grocery store giving advice on just about every topic: finances, relationships, job, family, health, weight loss, yoga—you name it. Yesterday, two ladies sat in the fitness club stretching room and for a solid thirty minutes complained about their relationships. One was giving the advice—loudly—and the other listened to her rhetoric. I became exhausted as a result of the conversation and finally left, because it was distracting, erroneous, frustrating and dominated the whole exercise room. *She would have gotten much further if she had just asked questions instead of pontificating!* I thought to myself.

Not many people know how to ask good questions any more. If people don't ask questions then they are likely giving answers, talking about themselves and not listening. And if they're not really listening, they're not being empathetic—and you can't fake empathy.

I became a better listener in my life as I engaged Pam and our children during the cancer journey. I really did want to see, hear and understand how each of them was doing as we maneuvered this cancer road together. I began to check in more often and tried to hear what was going on inside them. I wanted to be sure I was hearing beyond their words to something deeper. I learned to listen to the answers, dig a little more with good questions and then listen again without jumping in with solutions or commentary. I did this in part because I didn't have any answers anyway, but it taught me to listen more actively.

Have you ever been part of a conflict in a relationship and said to that person, "You are not hearing what I am trying to say!"? All of us have experienced those words at one time or another. I wanted to be sure I understood the story behind the story and didn't make assumptions about what Pam and our children were saying.

"If this chemotherapy does not work, Rick, I want you to find a new wife," Pam said to me late one night as we lay in bed talking. I wanted to plug my ears. "Pam, I don't want you to talk like that!" I said, horrified that she would voice that thought. "It's okay," she said. "I know you, Rick. You won't survive very well without a good woman in your life." She smiled knowingly. "And do it sooner rather than later." I wanted so much to stop that conversation because it was hard to imagine my life without her. But I needed to just listen to what she was saying from deep within her heart and I needed to hear what she was thinking about.

She was thinking about me. She was worried about me and our children and my life more than she was about her own. She had been living with this cancer for over three years at this point and had plenty of time to contemplate her future. She was able to place her days and life in the hands of God—and me with it.

"Pam, I can't imagine living my life without you," I protested. "It's okay," she said, "we're together now, but I just wanted you to know what I was feeling." I cried and hugged her tightly.

I used to think I was a good listener, but what I noticed was that I could improve my listening skills by actually hearing what was *behind* the words by asking questions and listening for the tone of voice. Those two things can often reveal something deeper and more poignant that the other person is experiencing. There is usually a story behind the story that needs to be told. People want to share it with someone they can trust—someone who can draw them out and is an empathetic listener.

So how do you engage people in real, authentic conversation? Through seven simple words: "Can you tell me more about that?" You can ask closed-ended questions like, "How are you doing?" "What do you do?" "Where do you live?" "What do you value?" Or you can say, "That's a really interesting tattoo. Can you tell me more about that?"

Maybe I should elaborate on that last paragraph.

Tattoos were never a part of my tradition or culture growing up in Canada in the sixties and seventies. So when it became vogue to have a tattoo on various parts of your body, I questioned their relevance. *Are people just trying to make a statement? Will this be a fad that will soon disappear? Some of those designs look a little scary—will those young people regret their decision as they age?* And I was not the only mid-life person asking these questions.

Then I went through an experience that put me in my place. It seemed quite innocent at the time, but it became a profound point of transition for me. Since then I have been on a quest to understand people's tattoos. Surprisingly it has opened up authentic and deep conversations with many strangers. This experience came at a point when I was trying to learn how to engage people more deeply in conversation. Here's what happened.

I was attending a very large conference for professional care-givers. I was sipping a cup of coffee between the sessions when I noticed a young woman with tattoos covering both arms. To my myopic perception she didn't seem to fit into this particular group of professionals and I said to myself, *Wow, I wonder who would go see her as a counselor?* Then almost as soon as I thought it, I felt a huge twinge of guilt and conviction for thinking it. *But you don't even know her!* I said to myself. *How dare you judge her without knowing her behind-the-tattoo story!*

I tried to track her down the following day to ask her about her tattoos, but couldn't find her. However, the thought of understanding people who get tattoos and why continued to haunt and inspire me. I officiated at a wedding that weekend, after I returned home. While waiting for the bride to arrive, I met with the bridesmaids. I immediately noticed that each bridesmaid had some sort of tattoo. Here was my chance to engage those young women and find out what the significance was behind each of their tattoos.

What I discovered was profound: one girl had a tattoo in remembrance of a father who had died the year before; another got her tattoo in support of her mother who was struggling with cancer; the third bridesmaid got hers in memory of a special pet. Within a few short moments, we had all shared some tears and joys as we remembered something very significant and important. I made a connection with those young adults by engaging them in the simple question, "Can you tell me about that tattoo?" It proved to be a powerful question — far more than I ever realized it could be.

So why is this important?

A healthy culture is based on authentic and open conversations that go beyond our individual ideologies and beliefs. We all have different values and worldviews, but we are all the same in that each of us has a unique story that is important and needs to be shared. Life is filled with stories: good, bad, heroic, cowardly, inspiring, sad, vengeful, hopeful. All of these personal stories are important to us and give each person an identity that is unique to them. You can't take away a person's story.

Now I take more time than ever to hear the stories of people in my world, my community and my neighborhood. Why? Because I want to let people—young and old, male and female—teach me about life. And yes, sometimes I want to tell my story as well, as I am in this book. And hopefully one of the stories found in these pages will be of benefit to you.

I knew Pam well, but I discovered deeper things about her because she was in a place where she had never been before. I really wanted to hear what she had to say, so I learned to listen carefully. In fact, as we traveled this journey together as a family, each of us in our own way became more empathetic. I would often catch our kids reaching out in ways that made other people feel cared for and special. Most of it they did by asking questions, listening, and showing kindness.

The next time you are with another person in a one-on-one conversation, try to plug into something deeper than their words and get behind their story. It's a really great way to live. The only problem is that you may have more friends than you can handle, because everyone will want to hang out with you when you ask, "Can you tell me more about that?"

CHAPTER 10
Fearful or Fear Less?

F-E-A-R has two meanings: 'Forget Everything And Run' or 'Face Everything And Rise.' The choice is yours.
— ZIG ZIGLAR

was seven years old and I was scared of the neighborhood's cat burglar. I had not seen him, but I had heard about him. The newspaper had written about this man who, late at night, would find an open window or door in people's homes, come in, and steal precious items. He was so good at it that he would sneak into bedrooms, taking pairs of pants with wallets in the pockets or purses lying on the floor. He would leave without anyone noticing. In fact, our next-door neighbor had found a pair of his own pants in his garbage can — the belt had been stolen out of them.

I was frightened. My bedroom was the only one downstairs, and I was by myself on the far side of the house. The worst part was that the only window in my room faced the back alley where the cat burglar was known to hang out. I remember being terrified and not wanting to go to bed for fear of seeing the perpetrator leering at me through my basement window. I would go to bed, and even though the curtains were closed, there was a small crack between them. And, oh, how I focused on that crack!

So I found a solution. I purchased a small pen flashlight that I would take to bed every night and hold tightly in my fist. I even had extra batteries just in case the others gave out. Most nights I would fall asleep with the flashlight on. My boyish rationale was that the burglar wouldn't possibly come into my bedroom when a light was on—and he never did. I was relieved when they caught him.

Fear comes from what is unknown and the unknown is what is in the future that's a wild card. Have you ever forced yourself to face a fear? When you faced it you realized it wasn't as menacing as you had thought. You got through it and came out the other side. You didn't let it stop you.

So what made you decide to face that fear? Mostly likely it was because it was limiting you in some way.

When you are diagnosed with cancer and go through treatments, you naturally think of the future. There will be some very real fears to face for sure, because there is so much that is unknown. We certainly felt those fears of uncertainty in our family as Pam battled cancer.

Unfortunately fear is one of those things in life that we need to work out alone. I don't mean you don't talk about it. But because fear is so personal, we can't ask others to face our fears for us—they are deep-seated in each individual. If you have a fear of flying, I cannot get on the plane and take your place. You will have to take your own seat.

I want to be honest and real here and say that sometimes your fears return at some level or intensity. Pam and I would face a fear one day, feel at peace, and then the next day, fear would creep back into our lives. It was a tug-o-war because of not knowing much about what was ahead of us. Everything was new and a little scary and dark at times. Doesn't fear feel dark to you? It certainly felt dark to us.

Why does the unknown capture us in such a powerful way? I think it's because we don't have a healthy understanding of hope. Hope is given a bad rap by the media and has gained a shallow meaning with very little purpose.

Think about this for a moment. When people say *hope*, what is the meaning of the phrase in which it's used?

- I hope that she will get better.
- I hope that the treatments will work.
- I hope that she will not die.
- We are hoping for the best.

That kind of hope feels very weak to me. Even when we say those words, we do not necessarily believe things will turn out well. There is already an attitude of disbelief and weak confidence for a positive outcome—a kind of "let's cross our fingers and see what happens"—as if an anemic god would somehow pinky swear with his pathetic, little creatures.

One day Pam woke up very frightened. She said to one of our daughters, "I'm really scared of dying." We had never heard this from Pam before. It surprised us on the one hand, and yet it was fair because Pam had never faced the real possibility of dying. She was facing the unknown and she was scared. Larissa responded, "You don't have to be scared, Mom. Remember, Jesus is with you and won't leave you." To some reading this, that comment might seem trite. But for Pam, it meant more than life itself. "Oh yeah," she smiled and immediately peace came over her. She was grabbing her proverbial flashlight.

Some people choose to live out of fear every day, no matter what their situation. They don't want to find the good in the world or in their circumstances. Their life is built on wanting what isn't, hoping that it will be and blaming others when it's not. Everyone is fearful of the unknown at some point in his or her life—we lie if we deny that—but we need to think about what it means to be "fear less" rather than "fear full" when faced with an uncertain future.

We learn about overcoming fears at a young age when, during the normal developmental stages of life, we begin to move out from dependence to independence, when we begin to step out into the unfamiliar and unknown. If our parents and caregivers have done their job well, we will feel secure enough to take healthy risks, knowing that we will be okay. This is key if we are to make good decisions in life.

Many of us have watched a child who is scared to take his or her first step, stepping out gingerly with uncertainty. But once they see their parents, encouraging them with hands outstretched, ready to catch them just in case they fall, they willingly take that step. The child is unconsciously thinking, "If Mom believes I can do this, then I can. I'll be okay." It does not take long for that child to overcome fear. And you know what over-comers do. The action that once made them fearful, they repeat over and over and over again just to prove they've overcome it. Why do we then become afraid of so many things later on in life?

"I'm scared" is a common phrase we hear from our children as they begin to try new things in life:

- I'm scared that I might fall on the ice and hurt myself.
- I'm scared to go to school because I might not know anyone.
- I'm scared to go to university because I may not be good enough.
- I'm scared to ask her out on a date because she might not like me.
- I'm scared to get married, because I don't have enough money.
- I'm afraid of having children because I don't have any parenting experience.
- I'm scared to go the doctor because he might give me some bad news.
- I'm scared to take a new job because I've never done it before.
- I'm scared to die because I don't know what happens next.

Our three-year-old grandson, Connor, became frightened by a short scene in the movie *Frozen*. It's the scene where the wolves are chasing Kristoff and Anna in the sleigh. It's the only scary scene in the movie among many other beautiful scenes, but that wolf scene was the one that had him waking up with nightmares. The concept was new to him. He had never seen a wolf before—especially one with big sharp teeth chasing down one of this favorite Disney characters! His parents wisely chose to put the movie away for a time. Then they gave him a flashlight (runs in the family!), a plastic statue of Jesus from his aunt, and a spray bottle filled with "monster spray" to keep the "monsters" at bay. It worked and Connor began to sleep through the night.

Much of our fear is a by-product of a world that likes to "awfulize." People are sucked into the vortex of sensationalism and the media seems to spend the majority of its time convincing us that we are part of a scary movie. "It's coming! Get ready! It's going to ruin you!"

That's what happened in 1999, as experts predicted the fearful outcomes of the year 2000 and that nasty Y2K bug that would crash our computers, cause planes to fall from the sky and create mayhem in the financial institutions. You couldn't buy a generator and the store shelves that once stocked bottled water were bare. People crammed their homes with canned food and toilet paper. People stopped living and braced themselves for the worst. Everyone waited for midnight to come and then...nothing happened. ATMs were intact, the lights didn't go out, and our computers carried on, business as usual.

How much time, energy, and money were wasted on angst and fear mongering over Y2K? Fear often becomes a time waster. It consumes us and takes away our joy. Who wants to live like that?

Pam had cancer. Did she live in fear? Did we live in fear? We certainly lived a life of uncertainty. Life in the future was unknown. But what I noticed is how we approached that fear. We faced it head on. It was not going to take away our joy. We refused to allow it to immobilize us as a family.

You can choose to run away from fear and not let it define you. It's a cruel master, though, when you allow it to run rampant in your life. The other option is to fight fear. But how do you do that?

1   Is there anything you can do about your current circumstance and the fear it brings? If you examine it and find you have some control over your situation, then do what you need to do to remove the issue that's causing the fear. If you have no control over it, face it head on and call it what it is.

2   If you begin to dwell on this fear too much, share it with a friend and ask for perspective. Be open to its reinterpretation and reframe it.

3   If there are people you are hanging out with who always live in fear, keep your distance, especially if they are rubbing off on you.

4   Decide what your "flashlight" needs to look like when you become frightened of the unknown.

Because I worry less about my future now, I have fewer unknowns. Because I have fewer unknowns, I have less fear. Because I have less fear, I experience more joy. This is not head-in-the-sand stuff. It's all about not running to meet a calamity and learning to live in the present.

One of the big lessons I learned during Pam's illness was the meaning of the word *hope*. A perfectly good word, it has been hijacked to mean something less than it is. It has become a nebulous spiritual sentiment thrown into space for the universe to answer. So I began to change my language and replaced the word *hope* with *believe*. Listen for the difference:

"I hope she will get better."	⇨	"I believe she will get better."
"I hope the treatments will work."	⇨	"I believe the treatments will work."
"I hope she will not die."	⇨	"I believe she will not die."
"We are hoping for the best."	⇨	"We are believing for the best."

There is a resolution in the word *believe*, a change of heart, an act of the will. *Hope* is fine, but unless it's anchored in something solid, it doesn't transform hearts and emotions.

I want to live a "fear less" life. How about you?

CHAPTER 11
Suffering Is Not Just About You

If there is meaning in life at all, then there must be meaning in suffering.

— VIKTOR E. FRANKL

B rian came to summer camp. He was in our cabin and he was a really great guy. We were a very competitive bunch and wanted to win the sports tournament. We usually tried to load the cabin with all the super-star athletes — we knew who they were from the year before. Brian was new to our cabin and to our camp. We noticed right away that Brian was born without one of his hands — in fact his arm only went down just below his elbow. While we liked Brian, we felt our cabin had lost its chance to win the sports award.

Our first competition was baseball. Before we knew it, Brian had taken his position as shortstop without conferring with any of us. We thought outfield would have been a better position for him, but didn't say anything. The first time the ball was hit in Brian's direction, we anticipated the worst — a man-on-base hit for sure. But we were shocked and humbled. When the ball got to him, Brian caught it with his glove and, like lightning, removed his hand from the glove, picked up the ball and threw it to first base for an easy out. We were dumbfounded.

What was even more amazing was his ability at bat. His first time up to the plate, he hit the first home run of many for our team and we went on to win, not just that game, but all the ones that followed. Brian became our ringer. He was our one-armed super athlete. I learned that day what it meant to compensate for what appeared to us to be a disability. It was no disability to Brian.

Suffering doesn't have to be a disability or a disadvantage. Depending on what it is and how we determine to interact with our suffering, it can become a catalyst that puts us on base and keeps us going around the diamond toward home plate. I have spent thousands of hours with suffering people, and so often I'm amazed at human resiliency. People fight through suffering because of hope for the future and something bigger than themselves. The late professor, Randy Pausch, said the following in his famous *Last Lecture*: "The brick walls are there for a reason. The brick walls are not there to keep us out. The brick walls are there to give us a chance to show how badly we want something."[2]

When people are suffering and dying, they are often fighting for some last moments to be with their family and friends. When people are struggling with cancer, they are often fighting for more days in the future.

After years of watching people die, I am convinced that people who suffer sometimes have more difficulty with their loved one's response to their suffering than they have with their own actual suffering. We don't want our families to see us this way and be upset. We are afraid to suffer, not just for ourselves, but also for fear of its impact on other people in our lives. And so we try to hide or dismiss it instead of living it honestly.

It works both ways. Family members don't like to watch their loved ones suffer, so they distance themselves because they don't like to be reminded of their own mortality and because they feel helpless in the face of another's suffering. I don't know how many times I've heard people say to me, "I'm not going to see Dad at the hospital because it's too hard for me." "I'm not taking the grandchildren down to see Grandma in the hospice because I don't want that to be the last memory they have of her. I want them to remember Grandma before she got sick."

Wait a second, who's afraid of suffering here? And who's teaching what suffering is and how to do it well and how to contribute empathetically to the one who is suffering? We can't turn a blind eye. Suffering is a part of life and pretending it isn't just cuts off the possibility of learning about ourselves and what it is to be human. This is so important. If you don't lean into suffering and invite others to be a part of it, then you are only thinking of yourself. Suffering must include others—we are built for community.

What do I mean by that?

When a person suffers, they do so from different parts of themselves. We are complex. We are created with heart, mind, body and soul. We may be strong in one area but suffering in another. As relational beings, we are called to help bear each other's burdens. If someone is suffering physically, we may not be able to remove the physical pain, but we can help alleviate that suffering by being present in other ways: relationally, emotionally, spiritually, intellectually. If people are left hanging in all those areas, the pain is unbearable.

Some people will appear strong and physically fit, but have a debilitating emotional disorder. That's suffering. Some people have a body that is deteriorating due to illness, but have an inner strength that is uncanny. I have counseled many people with a variety of problems. I always try to determine with them in what areas of their life they are experiencing suffering and then help them discover what areas of their life are strong and vibrant. Many find this approach empowering because then it's not all about the pain, but also about what they are bringing to the table to begin with.

I have not had cancer. I don't know the physical pain of experiencing tumors growing in my body. Pam did. Her mantra was always, "I do not have to suffer alone. I have my family, my friends, my church community and I have God." She invited us to participate in her suffering as much as she could. It was a privilege, because we watched her courage in the midst of it.

A church member phoned me one day and said he couldn't be with his dad. "I just can't visit with him at the hospice. I want to remember him when he was healthy." His father was suffering with a terminal illness, so I went to sit with him for a bit. He was sleeping off and on, but at different moments he would wake up and see me sitting beside him. I smiled and held his hand. Then I asked him if there was a family member whom he'd like to have visit him. "My son," he said. "He hasn't been here yet and I want to talk to him while I'm still able." I phoned his son again and convinced him to come. Father and son spent the next three days together. He was also there to watch his dad take his last breath. He commented later how fortunate he had been to be there with his dad in his final hours.

People have a difficult time watching another person suffer. But it's a part of life to share in someone's suffering. The son was adding to the emotional and relational suffering of his dad by not being present initially. The end result of his son coming to visit and be with his dad was beautiful—for both of them.

We not only live in a death avoidance culture, but a suffering avoidance culture. There is a drug available for almost any kind of suffering we encounter. We do not want to feel our own pain or see anyone around us experience pain either. As a grief counselor, I have experienced this over and over again. As soon as someone feels grief because of a death, they go for help and are given an anti-depressant to cope. It's as if sadness should not be experienced. Is sadness an inappropriate response to death? No, it's normal. That's an emotion that must be experienced. Unless you feel it, you can't move forward.

There is some suffering that we will have to endure by ourselves. And then there is suffering that can be carried with others.

Pam's tumors were growing and they needed to insert a tube into her abdomen. As the liquid inside built up, the pressure became so intense that we would have to drain the diseased fluid out into a bucket. So in the middle of the night, she would turn over on her side to the edge of the bed and I would help drain the liquid out to give her some relief. I was not the one suffering physically. Pam was.

In the middle of those nightly encounters, I looked deeply into her eyes and told her how proud I was of her and how much I loved her. Sometimes I would cry. Sometimes we would just hold each other close. What amazed me was that, even though she was suffering physically, everything else about her was not suffering, but growing stronger. Spiritually, she was a rock. Relationally, we were falling in love even more. Conversations were deeper than ever before and Pam's mental state was clear. In what areas of her life was she really suffering and in what areas of her life was she strong, vibrant and growing?

Let's consider suffering from a holistic point of view. What kinds of suffering should we be aware of in life?

Physical Suffering

Physical suffering is the most obvious type of suffering because others can see it — it's more material. You have heard the term "pain level" or "pain tolerance." Medical professionals will ask, "On a scale of 1 to 10, what is your pain level?" We honor the physical suffering of each individual without judgment because we can empathize with the pain.

Mental suffering

Simply put, our brain is a delicate balance of chemistry, neural pathways and connections. When any of these are out of whack, we experience suffering and process information that comes into our lives in ways that aren't helpful.

Spiritual suffering

Deep anger and despair directed toward God represent a unique suffering that leaves us feeling detached from a higher power and from something bigger than ourselves. Our soul searches for light in the midst of darkness and our hearts harden as we make ourselves the center of our own universe.

Emotional suffering

Re-occurring negative emotions (like anger, guilt and self-hatred) that leave us exhausted and at odds with ourselves and others can drive us into depression. Who knew that the beloved Robin Williams who warmed our hearts and made the world laugh was crying inside?

Relational suffering

People suffer because of relationships that are no longer there, are toxic, unhealthy or abusive. If a person does not recognize and come to terms with this suffering (and perhaps set healthy boundaries), they continue to live with an unhealed wound that impacts their life and the lives of those around them.

Suffering from purposelessness

"Why am I here?" "What is my purpose?" "What makes my life and contribution to this world significant?" When someone suffers from a loss of identity and purpose in life, they lose sight of all the possibilities for their life.

Suffering past losses

Many people do not recognize this deep suffering because it's so hidden and can masquerade as other issues. We can suffer from something that was taken away from us unexpectedly and has not been grieved or processed in a healthy and productive manner. This is called *complicated grief.*

Beware of attributing the word *suffering* only to the physical. We might be suffering in multiple areas in our lives or not, but operating out of our areas of strength helps us compensate for those areas in which we are suffering and keeps us moving forward.

I am so thankful for what I learned about suffering from Pam because it has helped me understand what areas are causing me suffering and where I'm still strong. It has helped me reach out and ask others to be part of my suffering when necessary and invites me into other people's suffering as well. This is how we function most efficiently as humans. John Donne said, "No man is an island." We don't need to go it alone.

That's why I say your suffering is not just about you. Nor is mine about me.

CHAPTER 12
Finding Inspiration in the Most Unlikely Places

I alone cannot change the world, but I can cast a stone across the waters to create many ripples.
— MOTHER TERESA

I have a few scars on my body. Each one tells a story. My most famous scar is from a championship hockey game as a 16-year-old goaltender. The five-inch scar that graces my left knee is a reminder to me of the greatest game in my hockey career. It still stiffens up during the cold winter months, but I'm glad it does because it reminds me of a great memory that I'm always happy to share with anyone willing to listen!

I was a 16-year-old hockey player in the North West Territories, playing goal for the midget all-stars at the Arctic Winter Games in Schefferville, Quebec. It was the final game for the gold medal (or *Gold Ulu*). For each of us 16-year-old hockey players from Yellowknife, the heat was on. The two remaining teams playing the championship game were those of us from the NWT and the team from Alaska. The game had quickly become "Team Canada" against "Team USA." We knew how significant that really was.

At the end of the first period we were up 1-0. All of a sudden, I went down to block a shot and felt my knee pop…and lock! A severe pain shot up the length of my leg. I could barely get up. I skated to the bench, dragging my left leg behind me. My coach said, "Where are you going?! Get back out there!" "It's my knee," I replied. "Finish the game!" he hollered. "We need you!"

And so, I continued.

We eventually won the game 4-1. I played in pain and as the team rushed onto the ice, tackling me after the victory, I couldn't help but feel more pain. We got to the dressing room and I took off my equipment. My knee was enormous and inflamed. The coach brought me some crutches and off I went to the doctor. "It's a torn cartilage," he concluded. We flew home the next day and the surgeon cut into me. There was no such thing as arthroscopic surgery back then. But that's okay. I have a big scar and every time I wear my shorts in the summer, I can tell the story of the greatest hockey game I ever played and the scar it left on me forever.

Do you ever wonder if there's a reason or a purpose for the scars of your life? Have you considered the deeper meaning and impact of what you've gone through — beyond your pain, suffering and dark valley?

It had been almost four years since Pam was first diagnosed. She had a few scars: four C-sections from having four children, two scars from her mastectomy, numerous small scars on her arms from medical needles and IVs. For her, they were all victory scars — symbols of overcoming something significant. I was proud of her. I was the only one who saw all of those scars, but Pam really did leave an indelible mark on most people she interacted with during her battle with cancer.

Pam went through many chemo treatments. The treatments were never just about her. She would choose people and ask them if they could be with her for the day, driving her to the hospital. No one ever refused to take her. In fact, I soon had a list of people offering to drive her to the hospital and sit with her during her day-long treatments. Often these same people would offer again and again, telling me how blessed they had been by spending time with Pam.

Once Pam had a bad reaction to her chemo treatment and ended up in the hospital for a short stay. It was then I discovered the ongoing impact and inspiration she had become to those around her, including the nursing staff that was taking care of her. I met a nurse out in the hallway coming in to see Pam early one morning. I recognized her and she recognized me.

She greeted me and said, "I'm so sorry that your wife had to come back again." "Thank you," I responded. "She is causing quite a stir around here though," she continued. "What?" I looked at her in shock. "We are fighting over her," she smiled. "Your wife is the most positive and appreciative patient I've ever met. All the nurses want her as their patient. They can't wait to go and sit with her. But I have seniority!" she said triumphantly.

There was a whiteboard in Pam's hospital room. Nurses would write a few notes on it as reminders. But Pam also wrote messages on the board—personalized messages and thank you notes to the staff and the cleaners.

I asked Pam if she wanted an individual room. "No, it's an extra expense and maybe I'm supposed to meet someone there," she said. Her roommates were always drawn to her because of her genuine concern, care and serving attitude. Even when she was weak or not feeling well, she would muster enough energy to help the person next to her.

I would often come to the hospital and have a conversation with her roommate. Over and over again they told me of Pam's kindness toward them. Pam would shorten that conversation as much as possible and feel embarrassed by the talk, but the person would continue sharing about how my wife had been so kind to those around her.

I wonder how many lives Pam impacted during her cancer journey.

I don't think Pam had any understanding of how many hearts she touched as a result of rubbing shoulders with people during her battle with cancer. It begs the important question though: What people have inspired you most in your life?

For me it has been those who have overcome a significant obstacle or circumstance and have come out the other side with a positive and upbeat attitude, living life fully.

- Do you get inspired by people who are rich and successful, knowing their wealth has been passed down to them from family members?
- Do you get inspired by people who won the lottery and are living a life of adventure?
- Do you get inspired by people who have achieved a PhD but who were gifted with an intellect beyond the normal person?
- Do you get inspired by people who get a great position in the company but then learn that a family member was part of the board of directors?

It's people who rise from the ashes who inspire me.

I get inspired by people who have dealt with unfair difficulties in their lives and still live life the best they can, with a positive attitude toward their situation, even in the middle of the storm. These people—the ones who do the hard work of life, invest in some dark night of the soul, take a few hits and come back into life with a few scars—are the ones who inspire me greatly. I want to hear their stories and learn from them.

I found a letter of reference from Pam's friend Michelle about her characteristics as a teacher and person. She says in her letter, "It is the underdog and the underprivileged to whom Pam tries hard to give assistance and credit. She often has them 'under her wing.' I know she makes a difference in many people's lives, but I know that it's most meaningful when she is able to help those who do not always understand things. To me this is a high standard and one which she is often meeting."

I noticed that Pam was inspiring people by being who she was. It's easy to live life to the fullest when you are healthy, but what if you're not? How do you live then? What do you show the world when you are not on the mountaintop but living in the valley? There were many people looking in on our lives—it was like living in a fishbowl: "How is Pam doing? How are you coping? How are the kids managing?"

One of Pam's friends, Elaine, had a cancer scare. Pam was in the midst of her treatments and she wanted to encourage Elaine, so she wrote a note. It is still pinned on Elaine's bulletin board at school. It reads:

Dear Elaine,

My heart went out to you this morning during worship. . . and I know it was very difficult for you. I wanted to wrap my arms around you, my dear friend.

I am almost packed for Florida [we were going there to get naturopathic treatments for Pam]. I still can't believe we are getting up at 4:00 a.m. and heading to the airport. I will pray like crazy for you and Paul—and for your upcoming appointment this week. God will go before you as always and guide your decisions in this. I will phone you when I get back and we'll talk. I send you my love and prayers that the Lord will uplift you and give you His peace. . . His COUNTENANCE that will shine upon you. I can really see that. Wow! Our faith is our compass. Thanks be to God.

In Him,
Pam (and Pastor Rick, too — I know he would relay his heart to you as well)
XOXOXOXO

:). . . it's going to be okay. God has revealed that to me.

We can't all be rich and famous, star athletes, world-renowned musicians or famous preachers to whom many look for their inspiration. Not everyone has super skills that place him or her in the world's eye where they can dazzle and be adored. Here is what I learned about inspiration as I took notice from the sidelines looking in on Pam's life: you don't have to have hundreds of links on Google or hundreds of likes on Facebook to make an impact on people. When you do a Google search on *Pamela Bergh*, you won't find anything except her death notice. She would never talk about herself. But if you were to ask the people in the communities where she lived, friends (like Elaine), neighbors and acquaintances, they can tell you the impact she had on them, especially during her battle with cancer. Isn't that the kind of impact we all desire to have on those who are watching us?

All of us at some point will go through an experience in life that is unexpected and unpleasant. Others will watch what we do and how we respond. It's at those times you can become an inspiration to others. It's not about being heroic. It's about being real. It's about having a ripple effect.

- All of us will get scars.
- How will your scar story impact someone else?
- Don't be scared to share it.
- Don't hold back something that can help someone else.
- Decide what you will do with the experience.

Perhaps the most difficult experience in your life will be the most helpful to someone else — something that will lift another person out of his or her desperation.

CHAPTER 13
Deeper Conversations
Most People Want to Have

*Let us make a special effort to stop communicating
with each other, so we can have some conversation.*
— MARK TWAIN

I sat next to a couple on the plane. The airline attendant had informed us prior to boarding that there were no television screens on board. They recommended that we purchase some reading material. There was also some reading material in the seat pockets in front and a husband and wife sitting next to me pulled the magazines out and, for the duration of the flight, had a conversation about the lives of the celebrities found in those pages. They knew everything about each one of the movie stars and famous personalities.

I thought about how sad it is to not have deeper conversations in our life and how we miss out on so much.

I do a lot of my writing in bars and coffee shops and, although I don't intentionally listen in on conversations, I am surprised by what people talk about and how shallow their conversations really are. People are missing out on each other and it makes me sad.

I must admit I have trouble with idle chit-chat—not because it's not fun or enjoyable at times. I recognize that we can't be dead serious or intense all the time. I'm certainly not in real life, but I do love learning what makes people tick and that doesn't happen in conversations about tabloids and movie stars. Isn't life about being taught? Every single person has something to teach us about ourselves, life and our situation. Why would I want to miss out on that opportunity?

I recently flew home from an educational symposium on *Depression and Grief*. A taxi driver picked me up to take me to the airport. A few minutes into the drive he said, "Were you here on a holiday or on business?" "On business," I replied. And then he asked me the question that I love to hear, "So what do you do?" "I'm a grief counselor and a thanatologist." "What's a thanatologist?" he asked. "It's a person who is interested in and studies death, dying and bereavement." He looked at me a little oddly. So I continued, "Do you have some experience with grief?" What a conversation ensued! In 15 minutes I learned this about him:

- His sister died by suicide.
- His father went into a mental institution following his sister's death.
- His mother died when he was 14 years old.
- He ended up living with an abusive uncle.
- He left the uncle's at age 16 to live with his grandma.
- He never married and he lives alone.

Each of these experiences spawned further interesting conversation with questions like: "Tell me more about that. What was it like for you as a child? How did you manage? Did that influence you?" For a moment, while I was in his taxi, I became a death educator. The most important part of that conversation is that we had a conversation about death, dying and grief. A conversation that was deeper than the weather, a sports team or the stock market.

We got to the airport and, as I was getting out, he said, "You are a good counselor." I smiled. I was about to pay him and get out of the taxi, but he continued to share more thoughts on the topic. As we were talking, the dispatcher came over his radio with another pick-up and he nonchalantly turned down the volume, not wanting to answer the call—so I listened for another ten minutes. Then I left.

People really want to share their story and I believe they are searching for safe places to speak about something deeper than their job, their kids, or their hobbies.

I know that my conversations began to shift with the ongoing uncertainty of Pam's disease. It had been over four years and we had gone back and forth with treatments and remission. I noticed that the longer we dealt with this cancer, the deeper our conversations became.

One night, Pam woke me up and poked me in the back. She said to me, "Rick, do you think I'm still beautiful?" I was taken aback by her question, but knew that it was important to hear her out. "Pam, why would you ask that question?" I asked. "Well, look at me," she continued. "This disease is really being hard on me. I can't even express my love to you, my body shape is changing and I have no breasts," she said. "Come here," I replied. "You are beautiful to me. I love you more every day." And I meant it.

"You're still hot to me," I continued. "I still remember seeing you for the first time, looking down at you from the bass section in the college choir. I noticed you and said to myself, 'Look at that gorgeous blonde hair.' And then when you turned around—wow—your smile, your good looks, and your beautiful eyes just melted me. Look at me," I said. "You are beautiful." She cried. I cried. We kissed and hugged and fell asleep together.

Conversations seem to change when death is staring at you. I'm not saying Pam was about to die, we didn't know. You always pray and believe for the best possible outcome. But the cancer journey placed us in a position to have some deep and precious conversations.

On another occasion she said, "Rick, what do you think heaven is like? Is it as beautiful as the Bible says? Will I get a brand new healthy body someday?" I knew what she was thinking and I really didn't want to go there, but I did. I don't ever remember having a more beautiful, deeper conversation about heaven than we did that night. I began to realize that some of the most deep and meaningful conversations that I had had in my life were the direct result of the most difficult circumstances I ever experienced.

I was 21 years old and home for the summer. Gramps was with us. He was dying and getting sicker by the day.

I was in the living room one night watching television and he was in a bedroom upstairs. I heard his weak voice call to me, "Rick, could you come here please?" I walked into his room and sat down on the edge of his bed and looked at his frail form. I loved him so much. For so many years he had supported, encouraged, prayed and loved me as his grandson. "Let's talk," he said.

Now up to this point in my life I had already had some pretty amazing conversations with Gramps, but none that would be as significant as the one that was about to happen. He reminded me of my heritage. He encouraged me in my calling and challenged me in my mission. Then he said to me, "And now I need you to pray for me because I am finishing my life." I grabbed my grandfather's hands and prayed the most difficult prayer I had ever had to pray, ending with "Thy will be done."

Two weeks later, he died. That deep conversation we had continues to uphold me when I feel discouraged and it gives me courage and faith to finish well. It made me want to live up to his vision for me. I want more of those types of conversations, don't you?

Unfortunately many people choose not to have these kinds of conversations or perhaps they don't really know how. I have always considered myself a person who likes to talk about the deeper things in life. But I have to admit, the conversations I had as a result of Pam's cancer were deeper and far more significant than any before.

I am more likely to have these conversations with others now, since I don't want to miss out on these golden nuggets that have the potential to impact and perhaps change some necessary parts of my life.

When you do a review of what conversations look like in your life, how would you rate them on a scale of 1-10?

1   I had a talk with someone in the last week beyond my work, family, sports or politics.

2   When I have visited with a friend over coffee, I have had a conversation that was totally void of gossip.

3   I had a conversation about an emotion that I experienced this week.

4   I had a conversation about something that I have never talked about before.

5   I took time to have a dedicated conversation with my spouse/partner that challenged something different in my worldview.

6   I had a conversation that started with, "I was wondering about…" or "I am curious about…"

7   I asked another person to tell me more about a certain point of view or perspective that I do not agree with and it did not interfere with my opinion.

8   I had a conversation that was extended because I said, "Tell me more about that."

9   I had a conversation at work that included, "I'd like to know your thoughts or feelings about…"

10 I engaged a stranger in conversation in order to learn something new about life that I did not know before.

I noticed that I was having more of these conversations, not only with Pam, but with my friends and family as well. I was reaching into my soul that was now thirsty for this deep talk. I wonder how many people actually find this oasis in their life.

CHAPTER 14

Making Mystery
My Life's Goal

*We must be ready to allow ourselves
to be interrupted by God.*
— DIETRICH BONHOEFFER

My brother Dan and I used to make tiny boats out of sticks when we were young and float them down the gutter next to our house when the winter snow began to thaw and the run-off began to flow. We would have races and a finish line. Once in a while, a gush of water would come and our boats would be swept along quickly in the current, sometimes so fast that we could not catch up with them and often never saw them again.

Do you ever feel like life is taking you to places so quickly that you can't catch your breath and you don't know where you will end up? I felt like that most days as Pam battled cancer. But I needed to understand and step into that mystery.

How do you make sense of *nonsense*? Cancer makes no sense because it can't truly be understood. No one can really tell you all the reasons for cancer. People who have done research have come to the conclusion that cigarette smoking can be a factor, the environment can affect it and the foods we eat can contribute. But nobody has all the answers to cancer prevention or treatment.

Nobody can break it down to assure each of us that, if we follow a prescribed plan, we won't get cancer. There are no guarantees. Across the top of Pam's hospital file, the reason for her cancer was given in bold black and white writing. It was this: "Pamela Bergh—a case of bad luck."

There are many things in life that are out of our control. There is something bigger happening in this life that we don't understand or see clearly.

Do you believe in mystery?

Do you believe that sometimes there just aren't answers to all the questions, situations and traumas of life? Let me ask you another question: How do you like being around people who have all the answers to your problems? Does it drive you crazy? It drives me crazy.

To live in mystery actually takes work until it becomes a way of living. Why? We are people who need answers. We need solutions. We need to understand. We want to know. We often live in a state of restlessness until we have an answer. Perhaps we do our best to make good choices but then life throws us a curve ball and we realize how small we are.

I was out sailing with our daughter Keeara one afternoon. We hadn't noticed the big storm that had moved in on us and we soon found ourselves in the middle of the lake trying to get back to our cottage. I tried a number of times to turn our catamaran around but was unsuccessful. The wind was so strong that I could not adjust the sail quickly enough. A number of times we were on the verge of capsizing the boat and ending up in the water. I kept trying to get the boat to come about, but finally gave in and allowed the wind to take us where it wanted to—across to the opposite side of the lake where we landed safely. I was fighting against something I had no control over. Once I gave in, it was a fast and easy sail.

A seemingly healthy person who has a heart attack might ask their doctor, "Why did this happen to me? I don't understand it. It makes no sense. I've always been a healthy eater. I've exercised all my life and then I have a heart attack!" We want to make sense of things.

I spent a fair amount of time trying to make sense of Pam's cancer. I'll admit that I still don't understand it and probably never will. I spent time, energy and resources trying to fight where the wind was taking us with my ongoing need for answers to my questions.

It's not uncommon for people to begin analyzing what went wrong when something difficult happens. That's being human. It's hard to keep on living without answers to our questions. And so we keep on searching and become frustrated, angry, or depressed, because we can't gain control or be satisfied with no definite answers to our predicament.

Mystery is about trusting in something bigger than yourself, and giving up your life little by little to the sacred or holy that is beyond your knowledge or understanding. The key then becomes turning your will over to mystery. Mystery is not a human endeavor to be understood, but a life that continually asks questions without a need for definite answers.

It seems backwards to ask questions without getting answers. But what I noticed from Pam's journey, was that we were in this continual pendulum swing, asking "why?" and "why not?" almost back-to-back. Those two questions were inviting us into something bigger.

What do I mean by *bigger*? The very act of asking those questions drew us into a place where the sacred met us in a new way. A conversation with the sacred can be powerful. Sometimes it's like a still, small voice. But that small voice can leave us significantly transformed.

I believe God does not treat us like puppets, but has given us free will. I also believe God wants us to ask "why?" so we can see the bigger purpose for our lives. Asking "why not?" allows us to move into life and its possibilities — it helps us to let go.

I have come to understand mystery as a wrestling match. Sometimes God wants to pin me down and sometimes I want to pin God down. We each want to make the next move. As we wait in between the moves, eyeballing each other, it is then we discover the beauty of mystery.

My good friend, Lucien, and I were talking one day about the uncertainty of life and how we do not know the future and how difficult it is to trust. Together we came up with this little saying that now sits on my office desk.

"What's given by God will come. Just let the river flow." (July 26, 2005)

CHAPTER 15
Small Poops and Little Farts

Laughter is an instant vacation.
— MILTON BERLE

love people who laugh. But people who laugh are not always happy. Sometimes laughter covers up something deeper that needs attention. We saw that in Robin Williams' life. He cracked me up so often, and yet made a decision to die by suicide. That was very sad.

I enjoy laughing. I enjoy hearing laughter. I have to admit that I'm a sucker for *YouTube* videos and *Just for Laughs* comedy that are crazy, slapstick and make me laugh out loud. When I'm having a rough day, I always find something to make me chuckle.

Pam was feeling pretty good and we decided that it would be a great time to take a trip to Hawaii. We asked our friends to come along and they agreed. As we arrived in Maui, we were hungry so we decided to get something to eat prior to checking into our hotel.

We chose a beautiful restaurant on the beachfront and made our way to our table. Robin said, "I want to sit over there underneath the tree." Our table was partially shaded under a beautiful tree looking out over the ocean. Robin, Fred, Pam and I took our places around the table. "Isn't this beautiful?" Pam exclaimed. All of us agreed. "I have the best spot!" Robin pointed out proudly. And then it happened. One of the tropical birds found the perfect spot to perch — on the tree just above Robin. It decided at that moment to drop its bomb and pooped all over Robin's beautiful sundress. We laughed and laughed as Robin found a napkin or two and mopped up the mess. Fortunately Robin laughed too, amazed at the bird's timing.

"Grandpa, you're silly!" Connor said to me. "Cows don't eat pizza! They eat hay!" I had been joking with him, but deep down I think I wanted him to enjoy being silly, too. I hope that our grandson, Connor, will laugh in his life or at least learn to use humor as a tool when life gets heavy or uncertain. He's already a pretty fun kid!

King Solomon was considered very wise. He once laid out an important list. In it he said there is a time or a season for everything. His list was extensive, but the phrase that most strikes me is this one: "There is a time to weep and a time to laugh, a time to mourn and a time to dance." We experienced all these verbs in Pam's cancer journey. These words resonated for us. But the laughter and the dancing were an important part of it.

Have you ever been around people who don't want to laugh? They choose not to include laugher in their lives. They're serious all the time. I confess that I can only take them in small doses. I really don't want to hang out with them for too long because they drain me of my energy.

Laughter is a choice.

I have visited many people in the hospital who are sick and worried. The infusion of a few funny thoughts or humorous tidbits invigorates them and helps them forget themselves and their suffering for a while. Of course, there's a time for deep conversation, tears and concerns to be part of the encounter as well. But laughter is good medicine.

When Pam completed her double mastectomy, we talked about breast reconstruction and decided she needed to be completely well before she went through such an operation. In time we would consider this option. It was important for Pam to feel attractive, however, so we scheduled an appointment to get foam implants and a special swimsuit in which she could feel comfortable.

I decided it would be good for me to go with her to this appointment. As we sat in the consultation, they explained the product they would be using. They let us feel the product. They explained how it fit into a special bra and swimsuit. Then they said they would do the fitting.

"Any questions?" the woman asked Pam. "No," Pam replied. "I have a question," I cut in and the women looked at me. "What's your question?" she responded. "Do I get to choose the breast size?" I smiled. Pam blushed, rolled her eyes and responded, "Oh Rick! Don't be ridiculous!" "Dolly Parton, Pam!" I teased. "Don't listen to him!" she said to the lady apologetically. "My husband's a little crazy!" She got her regular size in the end. Sometimes you make the best of a difficult situation when you add a little laughter.

Cancer is not funny — it's not a laughing matter. But what I noticed was that humorous experiences and stories found their way into our lives despite the pain the cancer was bringing. They helped lighten our spirits and lifted the heaviness. How do you lighten up when something is trying to bring you down? Find humor in the little things of life.

As Pam continued to recover from her chemotherapy, she noticed that the many chemicals and drugs she was taking for pain and discomfort were affecting her regular bowel movements. That was certainly not easy for her. You don't think about those kinds of things until they cause pain and bloating, but it was a real problem.

Then early one morning, as I was eating breakfast, I heard Pam yell from the bathroom: "This is awesome guys! Come and look!" We ran into the bathroom to find Pam staring down into the toilet. "Whoot! I did it!" she said smiling. And there, floating in the toilet, was a tiny, little poop the size of a peanut. She started to laugh. The girls gave her high fives and we hugged her. Pam beamed and continued to laugh and we laughed, too. Pam knew the importance of laughter and she knew the importance of sharing it with us.

I'm just wondering if we underrate laughter in our lives. I learned to consider its importance and effectiveness in helping us heal each day in the dregs of life that wanted to take us down.

Real humor is not a cover-up for something deeper that we're lacking. Instead, it brings a little sweetness and makes things more bearable.

Perhaps you may not appreciate potty humor — it's a guy thing, I guess. But farting was part of our everyday life, at least for the three boys of the family. I don't know what it is about guys, but the louder we fart, the prouder we get. Yeah, I know we are pretty shallow. Pam and our daughters would protest in disgust when one of us would let one rip. "Oh! Gross!" they would say to the perpetrator. Of course, my sons or I would laugh out loud and say, "Good one, Dad!" or "Not bad, Devon!" or "Saving that one up for a while, Landon?" We couldn't help it...

Because Pam's body was constantly fighting the disease and her digestive system was out of whack, she didn't always have control of everything that was stirring inside. I will never forget the day when all of us were sitting at the dinner table. Getting up from her chair, Pam let one go unexpectedly — it was a little 'puff' but audible just the same. She smiled. We laughed. "Good one, Mom!" we howled.

Have you laughed at yourself today?

Have you laughed with someone else today?

Have you found something to laugh about today?

You need to laugh today.

Find some humor.

Puff!

CHAPTER 16
An Entrepreneur's View of Cancer

*Leadership is not about titles, positions or flowcharts.
It is about one life influencing another.*
— JOHN C. MAXWELL

The snow was quickly melting and my older brother, Dan, and I knew that timing was everything. We had always managed to beat the other kids to it every year for three years running.

We checked the condition of the ditches. There was still a little snow left in them, but it was melting. We asked Dad about the weather for the next few days, and he told us that Friday was supposed to be very warm. We knew we had to position ourselves in order to have the advantage.

My brother and I would be the first to clear the ditches of the discarded bottles that had collected there over the winter. Bottles that drivers and passengers had carelessly tossed out of their car windows. They represented a wealth of bottle deposit money waiting to be collected. And who better to collect it than us!

We found four gunnysacks in the garage and checked for holes in the bottoms. We each took two. Mom helped us pack a lunch for the day, which we carried in our respective green knapsacks. At five a.m. the next Saturday morning, we woke up and had breakfast before Dad drove us down the highway. He dropped us off at a spot not too far away so we could walk back toward home, filling our sacks with glass bottles of all shapes and sizes.

We soon discovered that this was an exceptional spring for us, as we filled our sacks quickly and easily. At about nine a.m., we stopped for lunch. "This is a lot of money!" I remember my brother saying to me. "This is a goldmine!" I grinned. We were in grades four and five at the time and this kind of money was a big deal for us.

We started again and went for another hour until all four sacks were filled to the brim. And heavy! And we were still at least an hour's walk from home. We had a "team meeting" and the two of us decided we would leave the heavy sacks in a grove of trees and camouflage them well. If we ran home, we could get Dad to drive us back to the spot. That way we could empty the bottles into the trunk, Dad could take them home, and we would continue our business venture and rustle up more bottles. We were clearly just getting going in our lucrative enterprise.

Later, as Dad pulled off to the side of the road and Dan and I ran over to the stash of bottles we had hidden, to our horror, we discovered they were gone! Someone must have seen us hiding them and stole them.

We were very disappointed, but we made a decision that day not to give up. That choice proved to be pivotal in my life. It would shape me and carry me through life to the present. It would have been easy to give up, go home, and call it a day. But we didn't.

We told Dad we would continue. We also made another decision—to go down a different road. It wasn't the main highway, nor was it paved. It wasn't even one that led to another town. It was a country road—dusty and uneven with gravel and potholes.

What we didn't realize was that it was also a road leading to a gravel pit where teenagers went to party. We stumbled across the site that Saturday morning about ten o'clock. There we found bottles upon bottles—we had discovered the mother lode! Within 20 minutes, we had filled all four of our gunnysacks once again.

But this time we walked home, dragging the bags behind us. We weren't going to let someone steal our bounty again!

Being opportunists, we changed our strategy. Why wait until the spring thaw and collect bottles only once a year? We found a friend who had an older sibling in high school. He became our informant and would tell us when the next Friday night party would take place. We'd go to the gravel pit early the next morning to pick up bottles from the previous night's festivities.

Often in my life, I have experienced tough times and have thought back to that day when my brother and I took that "road less travelled." Had we decided to give up, not try a new road, or stop because we were discouraged, we never would have experienced all the good that was in store for us.

I still think of that experience when I run up against obstacles today. Ditch a ditch and find a new road. You never know where it may lead you.

Pam was the furthest thing from a businesswoman—that was just not in her personality. Once in a while I would try to get her to help me in a business venture, but she was not interested. She looked over my written materials because she was excellent at the English language, but not really excited about business.

But she was a successful entrepreneur. How is that?

According to *Wikipedia*'s article on entrepreneurship, a successful entrepreneur needs to lead in a "positive direction," using "proper planning" and be able to "adapt to changing environments" while "understanding their own strengths and weaknesses." Pam didn't run a business, but she was taking care of business in a positive manner and, through proper planning and brilliant adaptation, she was able to do just that.

In so many ways, she went down a different and unknown road and discovered a new way of living when the old way had once enjoyed had been stolen from her. She was successful and I wanted to learn from her and this is what I noticed:

1   She faced the situation head on.

2   She never blamed anyone.

3   She took responsibility for the next steps.

4   She was positive with all who helped her.

5   She lived and valued each day fully.

6   She invited people into her experience.

7   She released people when necessary.

8   She understood her limitations.

9   She showed courage.

10   She was vulnerable and authentic.

11   She always said, "Thank you."

12   She said, "Why not me?"

13   She trusted in a higher power.

14   She asked for help when necessary.

15   She shared her insights and her heart.

16   She was humble.

17   She cheered other people on even in the midst of her own pain.

18   She said, "What's next?"

These 18 different ideas came out of one cancer experience — perhaps one of the most difficult challenges any person can face. I learned a lot by taking notice of them and I think of them when I am making any business decision today.

Thank you, Pam. You are an inspiration and a closet entrepreneur.

CHAPTER 17
A New Kind of Love That's Even Deeper

Love goes very far beyond the physical person of the beloved.
— VIKTOR E. FRANKL

As I end this book, please allow me to share my love story as it unfolded.

I want to start with the topic of sex.

Sex should be an integral part of any marriage relationship and Pam and I enjoyed expressing our love for each other through this gift.

When someone goes through cancer, there are huge adjustments to be made. You begin to adapt to the new "now"– a significant transition, depending on the relationship you have with that person. One adjustment between couples is the role of sex in their relationship.

Pam was the only woman I had ever made love with and I was now missing something very special in my life. Pam, too, expressed how difficult this sudden loss of physical intimacy was in our marriage relationship. We both missed the lovemaking and longed for it once again.

We had children two years into our marriage and, as many of you know, raising children takes a lot of time and energy. It seemed as though we had gradually begun to spend more "alone time" together as the kids were getting older and more independent. We looked forward to being able to take couple vacations and getaways without the kids. We knew that as the kids grew up, we would be able to sleep in, cuddle together in bed longer, talk, caress, pray together and share our bodies and souls with each other—creating beautiful intimacy as husband and wife.

Pam was a beautiful woman and, despite her baldness and bodily changes, she was still attractive to me. And yet, I knew it was difficult for her to offer herself to me in this way.

When you are going through cancer, your body is changing. The ingesting of chemicals via chemotherapy does a big number on your system. Not only do you feel sick, but your internal functions are compromised as well. The chemicals just dry you up.

I felt so badly for Pam. What we enjoyed as husband and wife, we had to put on hold. As Pam continued to have her treatments and take her numerous medications, it impacted her body even more.

When Pam was told she had cancer, she was 43 years of age and I was 44. We were still in the prime of our sexual lives. Once Pam was diagnosed, it was very difficult for me to not make love with my wife. That one very intimate exchange with each other was greatly missed.

The expression of love through the sharing of one's body is such an intimate and special moment and it stopped. Cold. Yes, during her recovery times, we were able to make love, but the drugs affected her body big time and many times we would try but would have to stop. I did my best to comfort Pam at these times, letting her know how much I loved her.

We had had an active sex life and it had to be stopped. *Damn you, cancer! You even wanted to take that away from us!* I railed.

I talked with a lot of other men who had gone through similar experiences. It helped me understand the intense guilt I felt at various times as the results of my personal needs. And it also helped me understand what I experienced as a result of being faithful.

I was always faithful to Pam, but I will also tell you the truth: my eyes, thoughts and sometimes even my words wandered to where they should not have and I felt awful, guilty and disgusted with myself. I did not view pornography, attend strip bars, read seductive material or solicit sexual acts from other women. I did not place myself in the presence of another woman by myself. However, from my perspective on marriage and my understanding of my commitment to Pam, I felt that I allowed myself to be tempted, as small as that may seem. Even words can lead to something unhealthy and I had to say to myself, *No, I will not go there. I can't.* And I'm glad I didn't.

Here was Pam suffering with cancer and I was experiencing lust for other women. It was a very difficult part of my journey. One night I spoke with Pam about it and confessed it to her. She understood my challenge and comforted me. I didn't tell her to make her feel bad. I told her because I wanted her to pray and support me in my challenge. And I wanted to be honest—because that's the kind of relationship we had always had.

As important as sex is to a vibrant and healthy relationship between a husband and wife, I began to experience something that was entirely unexpected: a new form of intimacy that I had not known before. And this really surprised me! It was beautiful. It was deep.

I've watched many couples grow old together and often they display a beautiful expression of intimacy.

Have you ever observed an elderly couple—perhaps octogenarians—walking down the street, holding hands? They have found a love, a friendship and an intimacy that I believe all of us desire. Please do not misread me—I am not saying they do not have an active sex life. After all, Charlie Chaplin fathered his last son, Christopher, at age 73. And the *Guinness Book of Records* names Les Colley of Australia as the oldest man to father a child just short of his 93rd birthday. So let's not assume that age and libido have a negative correlation!

Pam and I came to a place where we had to put the sexual part of our relationship on hold. When that happened, I noticed it began to be replaced by a love that was much deeper than ever before. Have you ever looked into the eyes of your spouse and been drawn into something beyond words — more beautiful and more mysterious? That began to happen more often without the sexual component to our relationship.

My love for Pam continued to grow as we surrendered that part of our relationship and were resigned to a new normal.

I am not saying this wasn't difficult, but I began to understand the implications of the commitment behind the vows I had made to Pam in front of our family and friends 20 plus years earlier.

There were times during Pam's cancer journey that I wondered whether she would live or die. I didn't like to watch her endure the pain and suffering of treatments and recovery over and over again. I would plead, *God, if she's going to die, let her die. If she's going to live, let her live!* I felt guilty when I thought that, but I wanted the best for her. And I probably wanted the best for myself, too. Then I realized that the best was for each of us to discover a deeper kind of love as a result of this cancer.

I noticed this as I watched my mom and dad live their life as husband and wife. My dad was dying and one day I was visiting him in the extended care facility. My mother was there also. They were getting close to their 50th anniversary and I loved watching them together. The older they got, the more intimate their love. There was friendly teasing. There was more holding hands down the street. It was so easy and so natural. They loved each other so much.

"Hey, Rick," Dad said to me that day in the care unit. "Could you get me a dictionary? I need it for your mom." "What?" I responded, perplexed. "She needs to look up the definition of a word. She doesn't seem to understand it," he replied. Mom was doing her best to get my dad to eat more food, but he wasn't interested—he was letting go, knowing his time on earth was drawing to a close. "What's the word, Dad?" I asked. "No!" he said, smiling at his wife. "Oh Gene!" my mom answered, shaking her head. They loved each other and were beyond taking offense at each other.

So were Rowlie and Edith. What 88-year old husband toasts his wife at every single meal with a glass of milk? Every time I would eat with them, Rowlie would say a prayer before the meal. But before we could begin eating, he would say in a resonant voice, "A toast to my beautiful wife whom I love!" He and Edith had been married close to 65 years.

Wow!

I think I really did begin to experience this kind of deepening love as a result of Pam's cancer journey. And when I tried to understand why, I came up with the following observations. Perhaps these principles would allow all of us to experience this kind of love sooner rather than later.

- Marriage means giving, not taking.
- Marriage means showing up in the sickness, because in the health it's easy.
- Marriage means commitment to only one, no matter what happens.
- Marriage means focusing on the other's needs and not my own.
- Marriage is deeper than you think, if you want it.
- Marriage is a promise forever, so hang in there and receive its fullness.
- Marriage isn't a contract, it's a covenant.

"I love you, Pam," I would whisper in her ear as she lay on her pillow. "I love you, too," she would answer.

Cancer doesn't stop you from loving. It may even teach you to love in a different way. I believe all those who were closest to Pam were learning to love in a different way.

Soon, however, we would have to discover that love also meant letting go of the one you love so dearly.

Pam tried to go through one more round of chemotherapy, but after two treatments and her body's rejection of the drug, she said to me, "This is enough, Rick. We need to leave it all in God's hands now."

It was spring 2008, and Pam was weak. Even just two chemotherapy treatments had left her exhausted as we came home from the hospital. "I want to go for a walk," she said to me. So I bundled her up. She did not have much energy, but she wanted to walk around the yard. We went to the back garden where she had planted some bulbs the previous fall.

As I held Pam's hand and we walked, she kept saying to me, "Aren't the colors brilliant? Look at the details of those buds and the flowers that are coming through the soil. Look at how green that grass is!" I didn't see what she was seeing, but I replied, "Yes, Pam, those are beautiful and vibrant colors." I wonder what was really happening inside of Pam as she gave over to trusting God and letting go of the medical world once and for all. Do things really turn a different color when we surrender our life and our will?

Not long after that, Pam and I had an appointment with her oncologist. They had been so good to us. The entire team loved Pam. I think she was the ideal patient because of her kindness and appreciation.

The doctor told us that her recent blood test indicated that the disease was still growing—and now more rapidly than before. They could no longer slow it down. Chemotherapy was no longer an option. They recommended that Pam be placed in the care of a palliative care team.

As we drove home from the hospital that afternoon, Pam said, "I want to stay at home. If I die, I want to be in my own home."

Pam had decorated the Cochrane house and made it special. I said, "Pam, we will take care of you. I want you home, too." It had been four years and eight months since her diagnosis. There were some ups and downs, but we had experienced life more fully than we ever could have imagined. What we learned is that the little things in life become the most important things and the cancer journey helped magnify what was most important.

Pam sat in church that Sunday after her doctor's visit. As always, she sat on the side of the church where the pulpit was, right in front of me as I preached and led the worship service. I looked down at her and, as always, there was Landon, the only one of our four children who was at home then, with his arm around his mom and his mom's head on his shoulder. I thought to myself, *Please, God! I don't want to give up. I don't want Pam to surrender to this situation. Those kids need their mom. This world needs this amazing person for more than just 47 years.* I could barely hold back my tears, but Pam's beautiful smile and gorgeous voice instilled hope in my heart. Her body may have been frail, but her spirit was strong.

I must admit that I began to look ahead and wonder what was to come. I think we all did—Pam included. We were surprised by how our lives had changed as a result of Pam's journey with cancer—the things we noticed in her marked us indelibly. But we never expected what her last three months of life would do in us forever.

In many ways, dying might be one of the most significant events in your life. Looking back, I believe that Pam knew how her death would impact those around her and we are thankful that she chose to include us in her final chapter on earth.

Notes

1   Stephen R. Covey, *The Seven Habits of Highly Effective People* (NewYork, NY: Simon and Schuster, 1989), 255

2   Randy Pausch

About the Author

The author of *Finding Anchors* and *Looking Ahead*, Rick Bergh was born and raised in Alberta and educated at Augustana University College, University of Alberta, and Saskatoon Lutheran Theological Seminary. He is a Certified Thanatologist (CT), a designation bestowed by the Association for Death Education and Counseling (ADEC) after rigorous study in the area of death, dying and grief. In addition to his counseling practice, Rick is an author and speaker and has been heard numerous times on national radio.

Rick's various career paths and colorful life experience have given him a unique vantage point in his work as a thanatologist, educator, counselor, speaker and author.

Rick's 30-year vocation as a parish pastor positioned him among people who were continually working out life as a result of normal and unexpected transitions. His practical approach to transition is a result of hundreds of hours spent with individuals who were working through their loss, both personal and family.

His work in the community over the years as a volunteer, sports coach, community counselor, educator and funeral officiant broadens his knowledge and experience as he engages people in their everyday challenges, listening and learning from their powerful stories.

His career change from pastor to businessman afforded him the opportunity to travel the world, expanding his awareness of cultural differences and universal truths in the area of loss.

Rick has taken his astute people and business skills and applied them to his work with his clientele, providing practical and effective approaches to his transitional loss work.

His personal journey with his first wife, Pam, who was diagnosed with cancer at the age of 42, dying five years later, has shaped his principles and understanding of loss. He and his four children searched for healthy ways to move forward at a key time in their lives.

Connect with Rick on his popular blogging website (www.intentionalgrief.com), where he shares his thoughts, stories and resources of practical approaches to loss. You can also check out his many other resources at www.rickbergh.com.

Rick Bergh and his wife, Erica, live in Cochrane, Alberta, Canada, in the foothills of the Rocky Mountains.

CONTACT RICK

To get the latest *Taking Notice* updates and resources, visit: www.rickbergh.com/takingnotice

Rick speaks frequently on the topics found in his insightful and practical book. He can deliver a keynote, half-day, or full-day version of its content, depending upon your needs. Please visit his speaking webpage at:

www.rickbergh.com/takingnotice/speaking

Don't Waste Your Stories
How To Turn Your Valleys into Roads

Your story is important – especially the valleys that have shaped who you are. This free booklet is filled with ways to help you turn the most difficult events and moments of your life into something much more.

Go to www.rickbergh.com/dontwasteyourstories

All of Rick's resources are available at www.beaconmountpublishing.com

Learn more about Rick's transitional loss principles at www.rickbergh.com

BEACON MOUNT

Finding Anchors
How to Bring Stability to Your Life Following a Cancer Diagnosis

If there is one book to give your family or friends following a cancer diagnosis, this is it.

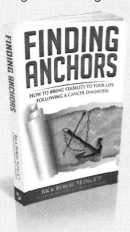

Rick Bergh shares the principles he has studied, taught and lived out for more than 30 years in this practical, inspiring and hopeful guide that will help anyone stabilize their life following a cancer diagnosis.

This book lays out 17 tried-and-true principles from hundreds of people, including Rick's own personal journey with his wife and four children.

Looking Ahead
How Your Dying Impacts Those Around You

The ripple effect from your dying has a huge impact on those closest to you.

During his wife's final three months on earth, author, Rick Bergh, learned 17 very important lessons. In Looking Ahead he shares a framework for you to consider so that you and your family can make the most of your final days together.

All of Rick's resources are available at
www.beaconmountpublishing.com

THE FINDING ANCHORS
DISCUSSION GUIDE SERIES

….reinforce the 17 ANCHORS with one or more from this series of interactive discussion guides.

Whether you are requiring…

- A resource to be used in your home with family
- A guide that will help form a community support group
- An educational tool to help your faith community become equipped
- Material to engage your clients in a counseling setting

…you will find a guide to meet your needs. For more details go to www.rickbergh.com/findinganchors/guides

FAMILY DISCUSSION GUIDE

FAMILY

SUPPORT MODEL GUIDE

SUPPORT GROUP

COMMUNITY STUDY GUIDE

FAITH COMMUNITY

IAL COUNSELING GUIDE

PROFESSIONAL

All of Rick's resources are available at www.beaconmountpublishing.com

Learn more about Rick's transitional loss

 BEACON MOUNT

51449395R00071

Made in the USA
Charleston, SC
22 January 2016